CW00493441

MOON ON A RAINBOW SHAWL

MOON ON A
RAINBOW SHAWL

A Play in Three Acts

ERROL JOHN

FABER AND FABER LIMITED

3 Queen Square

London

First published in 1958
by Faber and Faber Limited
3 Queen Square, London WC1N 3AU
Second edition 1963
Reprinted 1971, 1975, 1977, 1980, 1981, 1983, 1985 and 1989
Printed in Great Britain by
Cox & Wyman Limited, Reading, Berkshire
All rights reserved

ISBN 0 571 05403 X

For
Sheila, Robert and Ju-Ann—
and also for Edie

This new, revised version of *MOON ON A RAINBOW SHAWL* was presented at the East 11th Street Theatre, New York, by Kermit Bloomgarden and Harry Joe Brown, Jr. on January 15, 1962. It was directed by George Roy Hill. The setting was designed by Lloyd Burlingame, and the costumes by Charles Gelatt. The lighting was by Jules Fisher, and sound by Gigi Cascio. The cast was as follows:

EPHRAIM	James Earl Jones
KETCH	Robert Hill ii
ESTHER ADAMS	Kelly Marie Berry
MAVIS	Cicely Tyson
SAILOR	Michael Barton
SOPHIA ADAMS	Vinette Carroll
OLD MACK	Melvin Stewart
ROSA	Ellen Holly
POLICEMAN	Ronald Mack
PRINCE	Bill Gunn
CHARLIE ADAMS	Robert Earl Jones
SOLDIER	Peter Owens
JANETTE	Carolyn Strickland
A BOY	Wayne Grice
TAXI DRIVER	Warren Berry

ON CASTING THIS PLAY

TRINIDAD is the most cosmopolitan of the Caribbean Islands, with a history dating back to 1498. Since that time the Carib and the Spaniard, the French, the Portuguese, the African, East Indian, the English, the Chinese, Scots, Assyrians, Jews, Venezuelans and other national groups have 'bedded' together to provide the Island with the greatest variety of complexions under the sun; racial types so mixed that sometimes in one family one child is as fair-skinned as the other is dark.

Therefore in casting this play one should try as much as possible to pattern this racial patchwork, the mixture being more violent sometimes in backyards of the type described in the play.

ACT ONE

Scene 1. Moonrise.
Scene 2. The Next Morning.

ACT TWO

Scene 1. Late That Night.
Scene 2. The Next Morning.

ACT THREE

Scene 1. Middle of the Afternoon.
Scene 2. That night.

Two delapidated buildings make up this backyard property of
Ole Mack's in the East Dry River district.

The wooden walls of one building are weather grey and
gnarled. The other, more pretentious, sports a veranda. It
appears more solid in structure and design, being part wood
and part concrete. The galvanized roof slopes, half winking to
one side of the veranda, progressing upwards into an upturned
vee, over the main body of the house. It stands on stone pillars,
and can claim the distinction of having once been painted. It
is even lit by electricity. Ephraim has taken advantage of this
luxury. An extension cord, plugged to the socket in the
veranda, trails across the yard through the lattice-work above
the door and into Ephraim's room. The cord—a naked bulb
fitted to its socket—is secured to a beam by screwed-in metal
braces.

The Adams' half of the veranda has been turned into a sort of
make-shift kitchen-dinette, accommodating a two-burner kero-
sene stove, a food safe, a table and a bentwood chair. The
Adams' curtains are white and fragile, while Rosa's are of a
pretty flowered chintz. There is a water tap near the side of the
veranda at Rosa's end.

In staging, we need see only that part of the veranda with
the doors and windows leading off into the two rooms. The
backyard playing area should lie between the veranda and the
projecting platform that is Ephraim's room. It should be pos-
sible to see clear through Ephraim's room into the alley be-
yond. The entire furnishing of this room need only comprise
a bed, bureau and medium-size metal camp trunk. Mounted
on to the platform should be a practical working window
and two doors. One door opening into Ephraim's room. The

13

other, hinged to the same support, leads off into the wings. Connecting wooden steps lead down into the yard.

People leave the yard by going up some stone steps, past two crumbling columns from which swings a wrought-iron gate that opens into the alleyway. A rickety wooden fence cuts off the view at back. In the evenings a street-lamp illuminates an area of the alley near the gate.

If he so wishes, the designer may suggest by minimum construction or a projected image at back, beyond the fence, a corner section of an unfinished three-storey building. Its structure should appear to be of steel and concrete surrounded by interlaced pieces of wooden scaffolding. When incorporated into the design this structure should dominate, like some tall phantom, the two lowly dwellings in the yard.

Act One

Steel drums, sweet and low, beat out a rhythm. The lights come up on a scene stark and grey under the flooding light of a moon almost full.

A trolley pulls up out on the road outside. And we hear two rings of the trolley bells as it moves off again.

Nearby a guitar strums—and the calypso singer takes over with a rousing, thumping melody. The drums fade, leaving the singer and his guitar to carry on.

Ephraim comes into the yard from the street and begins to unbutton his khaki shirt as he walks down towards the pipe. The shirt is damp with sweat after a hard, hot day. He turns on the tap, swills his mouth out—then drinks thirstily. Removing his cap he allows the cool water to run over his face and neck. He straightens up—stretches—trying to relax his sweat-tight body. He steps up on to the porch and stands for a moment outside Rosa's door.

The calypso singer's voice swells to the rhythm of the guitar, and 'Epf' smiles as the words come across the yard to him. He comes back down into the yard and walks towards the gate and calls to Ketch.

EPF. Ketch!

KETCH. Eh-heh. Yer home, boy? I didn't know.

EPF. I just come in.

KETCH. It hot, eh?

EPF. Like hell!

KETCH. The night like it burnin' up, boy.

EPF. Yer tellin' me! I like yer song.

KETCH. Yer like it?

The Adams' baby cries out suddenly and Ephraim lowers his voice. Dogs bark in an alley close by.

15

EPF. Fer so!

KETCH. Is a new one I jest workin' on.

EPF. Carriso, fer so!

KETCH. Thanks, pal.

The guitar strums again and Ketch goes on with his song.

Ephraim recrosses the yard towards his own room. He switches on the light as he enters. The glow from the naked light bulb reveals, among other necessary furniture in the room, a large multi-coloured shawl lying at the foot of the bed.

The baby is crying again. He squeals and screams. Ketch has stopped his singing—Only the guitar is heard—it stops altogether some moments later.

EPF [*calling*] Esther! . . . [*He goes to the door*] Esther!

ESTHER. Yes, Ephraim.

EPF. You alone home?

ESTHER. Yes.

EPF. Why the baby crying so?

ESTHER. I don't know. I wish my Ma would come.

Esther comes to the door. A pretty, almond-eyed, creole girl of twelve. Brown in the sun. Two long plaits are held together by a pink ribbon. She wears a cotton print night-dress. Alert and intelligent, she has a funny way of throwing her head back and smiling, whenever she is happy—or just pleased about something.

EPF. Where is she?

ESTHER. She went out.

EPF. Then the baby must be hungry then.

ESTHER. I gave him his feed, Epf—He's just fretful—I wish Ma would come.

EPF. Is kind of hot tonight. I suppose is the heat.

ESTHER. Suppose.

EPF. Bring him out let him get some air.

ESTHER. This time of night, Epf?

EPF. Go on, bring him. A little fresh air ent go kill him.

ESTHER. Awright.

She goes in.

16

Ephraim remains at the door.

Mavis and a young American Sailor come into the yard from the street. She is a thin, wiry young woman—dressed in a blue bodice, hand painted skirt and rope-soled sandals. She looks up to flash a smile at Epf.

MAVIS. Yer awright?

EPF [*playfully*] Umm.

SAILOR. Hi, Bud!

EPF. Hi!

MAVIS. Go inside.

Sailor starts toward Ephraim's door.

No! Not that one . . .

[*Indicating her door*]

That one . . .

As the Sailor goes in, she makes a mocking gesture at Epf before she follows the Sailor inside. The light in her room is turned on.

Esther reappears with the Baby bundled in his bed-clothes. The Baby has stopped crying. She hugs him close—cooing softly.

ESTHER. Sweet, sweet little brother. Who's my soft sweet little brother? Who's so sweet, so sweet, so sweet? He's laughing.

EPF. Here. Let me take him. . . . Oh—he's gettin' to be a big man. And what's fer you, big fella? Yer want a slice of that ole orange moon? Look at it! See how bright it is tonight? So bright! Hardly a star you can see!

ESTHER. Full moon tomorrow night, Epf.

EPF. It looks so. Tell me, nah—all-yer decide on a name for this little stinker yet?

He sits on the porch.

ESTHER. No. Ma wants to christen him David Hamilton Adams —but Daddy wants to call him Churchill Spenser.

EPF. Churchill Spenser, eh!—Boy!—A little fella like you— with a name like that couldn't go wrong. What yer say? Man—I could see you awready as a member of the Ledgeco —making big speeches about grapefruit and cocoa-beans and compulsory higher education. What yer say? . . .

17

ESTHER. John Byron Adams—I wish they'd call him.

EPF. What?

ESTHER. John Byron. And when he grows up—he'll write poetry.

She comes down the steps into the yard.

You know what Miss said?

EPF. Umm?

ESTHER. She said if ever I entered for it I could win the Moreira Trophy for reciting.

EPF. Yer could, too.

ESTHER [*looking at the moon*] The moon is a stone. Did you know that, Epf? A man with a lantern in the moon! I want to know the truth.

EPF. Plenty of time for truth. Whatyer say, little fella, what yer say?

ESTHER [*on the bench, her arms thrown wide, recites with juvenile abandon*]

'Now am I a tin whistle,
Thru which God blows.
And I wish to God—I were a trumpet—
And why, God only knows.'

There is a pause.

EPF. No more?

ESTHER [*coming down to earth*] No.

Laughing—she jumps down from the bench and goes over to sit beside Ephraim. She puts her head against his knee. From Mavis's room comes sound of music played on a victrola.

SAILOR'S VOICE [*off*] Come on, baby!

There is a burst of laughter from Mavis's room. Esther looks up shyly.

EPF. Now am I a tin whistle!

ESTHER. It's a quatrain. Miss wrote it on the blackboard at the end of last term. . . . It's only three weeks to my first term at High School, Ephraim—and it looks as if I won't be going.

EPF. How yer mean?

ESTHER. So many things we find we have to get.

18

EPF. How yer mean?—So many things to get. When yer win a scholarship—I thought the government gave yer most everything.

ESTHER. Books—yes. But uniforms and other things you have to get yerself.

EPF. Oh! . . .

Mavis pushes open her door—comes down the steps and crosses towards the pipe. She is now dressed in an old imitation silk kimono.

SAILOR [*from inside*] Don't be too long, baby!

MAVIS. Cool yerself, Joe! . . . O God—It makin' hot tonight, eh, Ephraim?

EPF. Kind of.

MAVIS [*as she rinses and fills a large glass tumbler*] What happening?—Yer givin' little Miss Precious Mind PRIVATE lessons? She is a 'bright-girl' I hear her mother say—so I expect she'll *learn* quick.

EPF. Cut that, Mavis.

MAVIS. Yer want to come over and make it a party?

EPF. I said cut that!

Mavis gives a short low laugh—as she goes back to her room.

SAILOR [*from Mavis's room*] Come on, baby!—Come on! I gotta catch a ship yer know.

Mavis says something—and there is more laughter. Music from the victrola floats across the yard. Mavis's light snaps off, and there is a scratch as the needle is pulled off the record —then suddenly everything is quiet.

ESTHER. I hate this yard, Ephraim . . . I wish Daddy was working steady—then we could find a decent place to live. Ephraim—You could help it—You don't have to live here!

EPF. I'm a man, Esther. It don't matter for me.

Pause.

ESTHER. Epf? . . . Epf—You working night next week?

EPF. No. Why?

ESTHER. There's band concert next Wednesday night—and Ma says she'd let me go if you and Rosa would take me. [*She*

19

waits for a reply. He says nothing. She tilts her head back to look at him] Can I go with you and Rosa?

EPF [*gruffly*] Ask Rosa. Maybe she could take you.

ESTHER. Why not you too, Epf?—If yer only working day. [*Coaxing*] Come and take us! [*Smiling up at him—Pause*] Ephraim—You and Rosa had a quarrel?

EPF. Where you get that?

ESTHER. Well, is that why yer don't want to go?

EPF [*a little sternly*] Now who put that in yer head?

ESTHER. Then why?—Yer won't be home?

EPF. Something like that. [*As Esther gets up and moves to the other side of steps*] Hey! What we so disappointed about? A little old band concert? You should be on top of the world. Winning scholarship. Yer picture in the paper. Yer make yer ma real proud.

ESTHER. She didn't have to make such a fuss! Just as if she couldn't believe I'd passed, until she read it in the paper. Daddy was so happy when Miss came and told us—he cried.

EPF. Yer know, Esther. When yer grow up—It would be kind of nice if yer could go away and study—on a Island scholarship or something. Come back—Big! Yer know! Make everybody respect yer.

ESTHER. I don't know yet what I would like to be.

EPF. Yer have time! Time enough to make up yer mind. God! —If I had your kind of brains! [*Esther reacts—delighted*] The things I would have been!

ESTHER. Like what?

EPF. Yer know—I don't really know. One thing I know!--I would of been something more than just a trolley bus driver. That I know. Eight hours a day—Up Henry Street—Down Park Street—Tragarete Road—St. James Terminus—Turn it round!—Back down town again!—And around again! O Gord!

ESTHER. I like to hear the hiss of the wires as the trolleys pass.

EPF. Hiss! To my ears them wires sound as loud as a howling hurricane. . . . But if the next few days go right fer me!—

Go right fer me!—Go right fer me! [*Suddenly he smiles and speaks to the Baby*] Go right fer ME, little fella!

ESTHER [*excitedly*] Epf!

EPF. Shh!

ESTHER. . . . He's sleepin'?

EPF [*in a whisper to the Baby*] Dream yer dreams little man. Dream yer dreams. He wanted a little air. That was all.

ESTHER. Epf! Tell me! . . .

EPF. Shhh!

ESTHER [*lowering her voice*] Tell me nah, Epf.

EPF. What?

ESTHER. They going to make you an inspector?—Is that why?

EPF. Why what?

ESTHER. Why yer said if the next few days go right for you.

EPF. Inspectors have to ride on the trolleys too, yer know.

    He smiles and puts the baby in her arms.

Sleep easy, little fella. [*He kisses the baby*] Grow tall in your dream.

ESTHER. Is after midnight, Epf?

EPF [*winding his watch as he gets up*] Close on.

ESTHER. Then Ma should be home soon.

EPF. I wonder if in bigger parts of the world—when the night should have a moon—it seems that close! . . . Esther—if yer have yer head screw on right—No matter where yer go— One night—some time—Yer reach up—yer touch that moon.

ESTHER [*quietly*] You think so?

EPF. I know so! . . . 'Night. Don't stay out too long. I see you all in the morning.

ESTHER. Awright.

    As he crosses the yard, she calls softly to him, 'Epf.' He turns to look at her]

Nice sleep!

EPF. [*softly*] Nice sleep, Esther! And remember, ask Rosa.

ESTHER. I'll ask her.

    Epf goes into his room, pulling the door behind him. He climbs into bed.

Mavis' light goes on, and her door is pushed open. The Sailor hurries down the steps and goes out towards the street. Mavis appears at the door dressed in the kimono. She calls after him.

MAVIS. Yer could of at least say good night!

SAILOR. Go to hell!

MAVIS [*running to the gate*] Thanks. I will see and don't take you fer company again tho'. Not till yer get a little more experience.

She laughs. The Sailor has gone. She turns as if to go back to the room, stops, and addresses Esther.

Ay you! Yer playin' spy for yer mother. Well, look good! Then go and tell she what yer see. But if allyer think Old Mack goin' ter give me notice out of this yard, yer got another thought comin'. The old man know too right when his rent good. Call yer damn mother—Call she! Tell she come and see fer sheself!

ESTHER (*quietly*] Ma not here, Miss Mavis.

MAVIS. Where she gone?—Lookin' fer man?

ESTHER [*as quietly as before*] Miss Mavis—don't say things like that about my mother.

MAVIS. Miss Mavis. Miss Mavis. My name is Mavis. I ent no damn school teacher!

Epf gets up and goes to the door; pushing it open, he speaks with quiet authority.

EPF. Look nah. Have a little respect for the child. She ent interfering with you.

Mavis runs her eyes over his bare torso.

MAVIS [*coquettishly*] Awright doodoo . . . . Good night.

She goes in, closing the door. A bolt snaps, securing the door on the inside.

Epf sighs. Shifts his body. Looks across at Esther. Smiles. And pulling the door behind him, he turns out his light, crosses the room and climbs back into bed.

Away in the distance the clock on the tower of Queen's Royal College begins to chime.

Esther sits with the baby nestling in her lap. She sings softly as the clock rings out the midnight hour.

Esther's song

'Do-do, petit popo.

Petit popo, n'ouvrir do-do

Do-do, petit popo.'

Sophia Adams comes into the yard from the street. She is a plump 'red'-skinned woman—in her late thirties. Hard times and worry have lined her, so that she looks somewhat older. She can be gay and frivolous when it suits her purpose. She can also be hard, unyielding—decisive. She is the backbone of her family—hence a bit of a bully.

She is wearing a shabby pair of black court shoes, and a button-through dress in a cheap cotton print.

SOPHIA. Esther!—What you doing out here this time of night? And is that the baby yer have with yer?

ESTHER. Ma?

SOPHIA. Child, yer crazy or what? Is kill yer trying to kill him. This is straight pneumonia, yes. Inside with you, eh, before I clout yer head off.

Esther scurries indoors. Sophia goes up the steps into the veranda where she begins a search of the food safe and the table drawer.

Nobody would think you is a child what win scholarship, the stupidness you does do some times. Yer father gone out, I suppose.

ESTHER [*from inside*] Yes, Ma.

SOPHIA. The moment I turn mey back that man disappear. So help mey!—Tonight—Tonight I will lock that door! He sleep out here in the veranda. Out!—Only God knows where —killing somebody bad rum. Yer can't find a thing in this place when yer want it.

ESTHER. What yer looking for, Ma?

SOPHIA. The candle!

ESTHER. It's inside here, Ma.

SOPHIA. Well, give it to me! Give it to me!

The door opens and Esther's hand appears with the candle in it. Sophia snatches the candle and turns to take up a box of matches near the stove. She lights the candle.

I wish you an' yer father put things back where yer find them. The time it take me to find the candle I could of wet myself.

Old Mack and Rosa come into the backyard from the street.

Like yer doing chauffeur work again tonight, Mr. Mack?

OLD MACK. Always ready to oblige, Mrs. Adams.

SOPHIA. I know!

Old Mack laughs. Sophia hurries off around the side of the house.

Rosa is eighteen. Nicely framed. She wears a dress of some fine-spun rayon material. She wears ear-rings of solid gold. A Cyma wristwatch with black and gold attachments. Brown leather sandals. Her speech and manner—simple—unaffected.

Old Mack is sixty-five. Dark-skinned, small and grey. He is well dressed—in an expertly tailored lightweight suit, hand-made shoes and panama hat.

ROSA. And did your son stay in England right through the war, Mr. Mack?

OLD MACK. Right through it. Now it looks as if I'll have to go up there and drag him home. Says he prefers London. I need him here.

ROSA. There is a big reception in the Princes Buildings tonight for the troops that return. I wish I had had time off to go and see it. I asked Stephen—but . . .

OLD MACK. You should have asked me, Rosa. [*He puts his hand on her arm*] Any time. Anything you want, Rosa. Any time. Ask. Is yours.

ROSA [*extending her hand*] Good night, Mr. Mack.

She turns to go.

OLD MACK. Not so soon tonight, Rosa. Sit down here. [*He sits on the edge of the porch*] Less talk a while.

ROSA. Is late. And is my turn to open the café early tomorrow.

OLD MACK. You let me have them keys. Take tomorrow off. The rest of the week if yer want. Let Stephen see to the café

—That's what I pay him for. [*Pressing close*] Make me some
coffee. Hot and strong.

ROSA. Is late, Mr. Mack.

OLD MACK [*going to the stove*] Fer coffee?—Is never late for
coffee, child.

ROSA. Mr. Mack——

OLD MACK. Rosa!—Don't yer like me?

ROSA. Mr. Mack!

OLD MACK [*crossing to her*] I been good to yer. Anything you
want——

ROSA. Mr. Mack—Somebody will hear yer.

OLD MACK. Come back to my place—Anything yer want, Rosa.

ROSA. No!

OLD MACK. [*close—as he tries to embrace her*] Anytime!—
Ask!—Is yours!

ROSA. No ! ! !

*She pulls hard—away from him. He stumbles and falls
awkwardly to his knees—his arms around her—his cheek
against her thigh. Sensual tears burn his eyes.*

OLD MACK. Rosa, every time I come to the café——

ROSA. Mr. Mack!—Let me go!

*She tries to break his hold, but his fingers are knotted in
front of her thighs. His cheek pressing hard against her flank.*

OLD MACK. I see yer, Rosa, I want yer. Most nights in the car
I bring yer home yer sit so close——

*Sophia comes around the side of the house, the candle
flaming in her hand.*

ROSA. MR. MACK—LET ME GO !

OLD MACK. Rosa! Rosa! Please! Please! Rosa! Please, Rosa!

SOPHIA. Well! Put this candle in his hand, and I would say
that it was the Baptist preacher giving baptism.

Her voice intrudes.

*He breaks away tugging at his tie in embarrassment. His
eyes are wild. He backs away from the women mumbling
inarticulate apologies. Then he tries, almost comically, like a
Chaplinesque drunk, to compose himself. He turns quickly,*

25

walking with a forced dignity, through the gate and out towards the street.

Sophia sees the panama, picks it up and rushes after him. Yer don't want yer panama? Mr. Mack! Mr. Mack! Look yer panama! (*Almost collapsing with laughter*] O God! O God!—O God! Well, look we crosses, nah! O my God, oohhh!

A car starts up and drives away.

ROSA [*coming down the steps*] Don't laugh at him, Mrs. Adams. Give me the hat—I will take it for him in the mornin'.

SOPHIA. Well, well, well! Yer mean is sleep he was askin' yer to sleep with him? Old devil. Give him a whole pot of strong coffee and he still wouldn't be able to make the grade.

Rosa takes the panama and turns away, her lips playing with a smile. The ear-rings dangle and glitter in the candle-light.

Ear-rings, girl! Let me see—Let me see! [*She holds the candle perilously close to Rosa's ear*] And solid gold too! Is from the old man you get them, nah?

ROSA. Just now before I close up the café.

She sits on the steps.

SOPHIA. Hm. . . . Ear-rings, wristwatch, new clothes and all kinds of fancy shoes and things you taking from this ole man—I suppose he right to seek his rights.

ROSA [*with spirit*] I didn't ask him to give mey them, Mrs. Adams.

SOPHIA. Yes—But yer wearin' them! Them nuns you grow up with—I think they teach you to look at life too simple.

Mavis comes down the steps and goes out to street singing 'All Or Nothing At All'. She laughs as she goes.

Damn little spoat! [*Then to Rosa*] Well, child all I could say is that you must be tickling the right vein in him. For in all the years we been rentin' from him—he is a man I never know to be generous. What is Ephraim sayin' about all this?

ROSA [*defiantly*] I don't see why he should say anything. In all the months I know Ephraim he never give me a thing.

SOPHIA [*teasing*] No?

ROSA [*embarrassed*] I don't mean that, Mrs. Adams.

SOPHIA. I should hope yer don't mean that. Because is for Ole
Mack so to hand out the expensive presents. Strong, healthy
young men have other things to give.

ROSA. Mrs. Adams, yer too wicked, yer know.
They laugh together.

SOPHIA. What time is it?

ROSA. Just past half-past.

SOPHIA. And that damn husband of mine still out. . . . God!
[*She sits down in the chair*] Sometimes when I stop to think,
eh, Rosa . . . Mey brain! . . . Esther—and school . . . Charlie
not working. The baby. I don't know, child—I don't know.
. . . Look—I better go in. I have a whole bundle of washing
to bleach out in the morning—So if yer see silk and satin
hanging on the line, child—Not *one* is mine. Night! . . .
[*And as she gets up, she looks across towards Ephraim's room*]
Yer tell him yet?

ROSA. No.

SOPHIA. When you goin' tell him?

ROSA. Soon.

SOPHIA. Well, you better. And soon. A girl like you with no
mother or father to look out for you. Tell him soon!
Sophia goes in.
Rosa remains on the porch, looking across the yard.
*Rosa moves down the steps. She stops a moment to remove
the ear-rings from her ears. Then she crosses the yard towards
Ephraim's room. Steel music steals in. Pulling open the door
she goes in. The bed area lights up. Rosa stands looking down
at the sleeping man. Then she sits down beside him, laying her
cheek against the curve of his shoulder, her arms caressing
him.*
*Epf stirs, and turning on his back opens his eyes. Rosa smiles,
and reaching over, kisses him softly on the mouth.*

ROSA. Didn't mean to wake yer.

EPF. No?

Rosa shakes her head. Epf pulls her face to his, kissing her hard.

Yer stayin'?

ROSA. . . . Yer want me?

He looks at her for a long moment before turning to lie on his side.

EPF. Go an' sleep, and let me get some sleep.

ROSA. Ephraim!

EPF. Go, nah!

The music begins to fade. Rosa gets up and goes out, crossing the yard towards her room. Ephraim sits up and reaches for a cigarette as the lights fade.

Act One

SCENE 2

The next morning. Children's voices as they play next door.

LITTLE BOY [*next door*] One, two, three. Mother catch a flea. Flea die—Mother cry—one, two, three! You to catch, Janette!—You to catch! Hoooop! Hoooop!

CHILDREN'S VOICES. Hoooop! Hoooop! Hoooooop!

And the stage is flooded suddenly with warm sunshine, becoming brilliant as the mid-morning sun burns its way across the sky. Sophia and Esther are half-way through their morning meal. Sophia, in a faded cotton frock and an old pair of her husband's shoes, which are sizes too large for her, is sitting with her back to the yard. She is nursing the baby. Esther sits facing the yard, doodling with her meal.

CHILDREN'S VOICES [*chanting*] Yer can't catch me tho'! Yer can't catch me tho'! Yer can't catch me tho'! [*Wild laughter*] Janette! Janette!

JANETTE. I caught yer!—I caught yer! I CAUGHT YER!

The Children laugh wildly, and over the laughter Janette begins to count—loudly and more deliberately.

One! Two! Three! Mother catch a flea! Flea die! Mother
cry! One! Two! Three!

*The Children are screaming with laughter as they begin
another game.*

SOPHIA. I wish those damn children from next door would stop
keepin' so much blasted noise this time of mornin'! An'
boy!—Come, come! Suck, suck! Suck nah, boy! I certainly
ent have all mornin' to sit here fooling with you!

Esther is about to help herself to something from the table.
You take yer hand from that. Is fer yer father.

ESTHER. But Ma . . .

SOPHIA. Leave it, yer hear me. Tho' it would be damn good
for him if he came in and didn't find any.

ESTHER. Didn't he come in at all last night, Ma?

SOPHIA. Yer ask too many damn questions, Esther. Stop
playing with yer breakfast. Yer havin' it late enough
as it is.

ESTHER. But Mama! . . .

SOPHIA. Yer hear me?

ESTHER (*directly at her mother*) Yes, Ma!

Ephraim, in bed, stirs and sits up.

GIRL [*calling from street*] Janette! . . . Janette!

JANETTE [*as she runs past, along the alley way*] Coo-oooooo!

ESTHER. JANETTE!

She runs to the gate.

JANETTE. Esther! A lot of police out by the corner. You want
to come and see?

ESTHER: Ma?

Sophia ignores her.

GIRL [*offstage*] Jan, less go!

JANETTE. We're coming, Laura!

*And we hear her as she joins the other children as they move
along the alley towards the street.*

ESTHER. Ma! Can I go and see?

SOPHIA. No!

ESTHER. But, Ma! . . .

29

SOPHIA. Esther! Don't make me lose mey temper with yer this morning! Them so over there livin' in big house. And they mother have servants to clean up after them. I ent have no help but you. Don't frown up your face at me.

Pouting, Esther stomps back to sit on the porch. And Sophia turns her attention to the baby.

Awright, young man—I think you had enough. Come. Inside. Sleep fer you.

Getting up, she chants a little 'nothing' to the baby.

> 'Pampalam-pa-likkeelee
> This little man don't love me.
> Pampalam-pa-likkeelee
> This little man going kill me.'

Ephraim lights up on a cigarette.

From inside as she tucks the baby away

Sleep fer you! Sleep fer you! The mornin's going!—And yer mama got a lot of things to do.

Esther sneaks out of the yard and past the gate just as Sophia comes back into the porch. Esther ducks down behind the broken piece of wall near the gate. Realizing the girl could not have gotten far, Sophia speaks without raising her voice:

Yer know yer have to finish the needlework Miss Jackman gave yer to do?

ESTHER. Yes, Ma.

Esther comes back into the yard.

SOPHIA. Yer goin' have to learn to use yer hands. Fer the way things goin' it look to me like yer ent goin' be goin' to no damn High school. Yer father? I trying mey best. Since seven 'clock this mornin' I up to mey elbows in that damn washtub. He going get such a tongue lashing from me this mornin' . . .

She breaks off as she hears the Fisherwoman call from the street.

FISHERWOMAN. Fish! Fresh fish! Get yer nice fresh fish! Fish!

SOPHIA [*calling as she comes down the steps*] Mai! Mai!

FISHERWOMAN [*offstage*] Lady?

SOPHIA [*looking out along the alley-way*] What yer got?

FISHERWOMAN. I got shark! Kingfish! An' some cascadoo!

SOPHIA. It fresh?

FISHERWOMAN. Yes, Lady. Is fresh fish!

SOPHIA. Yer sure it fresh?

FISHERWOMAN. Yesss!

SOPHIA. Then you could keep it! I ent want no fish today!

The Fisherwoman swears in Hindustani.

SOPHIA [*coming back into the yard*] And the same to you!

FISHERWOMAN. Damn Nega!

SOPHIA (*wheeling around to shout up the alley-way*) Coolie! Twice
in the last three weeks you sell me rotten fish! Yer damn
thiefing Coolie! When yer get the fish what the hell yer does
do with it? Keep it under yer bed?

*Rosa, dressed in a striped linen, is laughing as she comes in
from the street.*

SOPHIA. Damn thiefing wretch! I did long have that fer she!
The damn Coolie!

ROSA. I really don't want to laugh.

ESTHER. Rosa—You going to band concert?

ROSA. If Ephraim's going. You all heard what happen, Mrs.
Adams?

SOPHIA. No.

*Rosa has moved up the steps to Ephraim's room. She calls
softly.*

ROSA. Ephraim? Ephraim? . . . God—He still sleeping. And
I wanted to talk to him. . . . Somebody broke open the café.

*Ephraim sits listening—but makes no movement towards
the door.*

ESTHER. Your café, Rosa?

SOPHIA [*as Rosa nods her reply*] No! What they take?

ROSA. Every penny, Mrs. Adams. Seventy dollars!—And some
small change we had left in the register.

SOPHIA. No! When this happen?

ROSA. Last night it look like. Police in there right now.

SOPHIA. And where Mr. Mack?

ROSA. In the café. I had was to telephone to tell him. He's so mad, Mrs. Adams—He could hardly talk.

SOPHIA. Pity they didn't carry way the whole damn café! By now so he paralytic with a stroke!

ROSA [*enjoying Sophia's reaction but still reproving*] Mrs. Adams!

SOPHIA. Thief from thief, child, does make Jehovah laugh! An' I is only a mere mortal. It serve him right. The way he robbing we here with the rent on these nasty little rooms. Serve him blasted right. Every damn night somebody should go in there and carry way something.

ROSA. And I'd be having to look for a job.

SOPHIA. You'll get one!

A young Policeman has come into the yard.

POLICEMAN. Miss Otero?

ROSA. Yes.

POLICEMAN. The sergeant wants yer back at the café.

ROSA. I gave my statement awready.

POLICEMAN. He didn't say yer could leave, lady.

There is a pause while Rosa just looks at the Policeman.

ROSA. I came to get something. Can I go inside and get it?

POLICEMAN. Sure.

Rosa goes into her room.

ESTHER [*as she follows Rosa inside*] Rosa, what the police ask yer? Rosa?...

Ephraim lights another cigarette.

Sophia comes down the steps with a bucket—goes to the pipe, draws some water and starts back up the steps. All the while, keeping her eyes on the young Policeman. Only when she is up the steps again does she address him.

SOPHIA. How old you is, young man?

POLICEMAN. Nineteen.

SOPHIA. Where yer mother?

POLICEMAN. Home—I suppose.

SOPHIA. She should be ashame of herself. Having a lil' boy like you playin' policeman.

POLICEMAN. I could take care of myself, lady, don't worry.

SOPHIA. For your mother's sake, I hope so.

Rosa reappears with Old Mack's panama hat in her hand.

ROSA. Oh, Esther. Don't ask so many questions.

ESTHER. I only wanted to know.

ROSA [*as she comes down steps*] Mrs. Adams. Tell Ephraim I'll see him tonight. After work.

SOPHIA. Awright, child.

ROSA [*to Policeman*] Come go.

SOPHIA. Rosa? Mind and hold the little boy's hand as soon as allyer get on the sidewalk—or he might lose his way.

Esther laughs loudly at her mother's remark. Sophia cuts into the laughter.

Esther! Is time yer start on yer needlework.

Esther picks up some of the dishes and goes inside. Rosa and the Policeman are gone.

Well I glad! I too damn glad somebody outdo that damn old miser at last! Lay up not for yourself TREASURES! God! —How I wish was me did pick out he eye! Now so—All mey troubles over!

Sophia sings joyously.

> 'There's no hidin' place down here
> There's no hidin' place down here
> I went to the rocks to hide myself
> The rocks cried out I'm hidin' too
> There's no hidin' place down here.'

Epf opens his door and looks out at Sophia.

EPF. Mornin'.

SOPHIA. Ay-ay! Beauty! Yer wake?

EPF. Wide.

SOPHIA. Funny.

EPF. What?

SOPHIA. Rosa was just there trying to wake yer.

EPF. Oh?

Sophia's door bursts open as Esther races towards Epf.

ESTHER. Epf—Yer know what happen? This mornin'
they . . .

SOPHIA. Young lady!

ESTHER [*stops*] Ma?

SOPHIA. Inside.

ESTHER. But Ma?—I only wanted . . .

SOPHIA. Inside!—Yer hear mey? Big people can't talk these
days but yer want to put yer mouth in it. Inside!

*Esther looks at her mother. Sophia says nothing. Esther
goes into the house.*

And don't let me ketch yer out here again unless I call yer.

EPF. She was telling me something.

SOPHIA. Oh—Last night . . . Somebody break . . . [*She stops*]
Ephraim—All this mornin' inside there—you wasn't sleeping?

*He turns back into the room for a towel and some toilet
articles.*

When Rosa call yer? . . . Boy—What tricks yer up to?

*And suddenly she begins to laugh. The laughter comes in
short bursts.*

No! Eh-eh! No! God! It would be too funny! No!

EPF [*as he comes down into the yard*] Lady, what's the joke?

SOPHIA. It ent you?

EPF. Me? . . . What? [*Laughing as he gets her meaning*] Lady!

*He turns away and moves down to the water tap where he
takes up a cake of soap.*

SOPHIA. So you was listening! Then I suppose yer heard Rosa
say she want to see yer tonight?

EPF. Umhmm.

He is suddenly quite serious. Sophia is looking at him.

SOPHIA. You up to something. What it is I don't know. But
I'd swear you up to something.

EPF [*on guard*] Something like what?

SOPHIA. I don't know. I was only pulling yer leg just now. I
don't think you would steal. Least not from Ole Mack.

EPF. Thank you.

He is crossing towards the shower.

SOPHIA. But if Rosa was my daughter . . . I'd be having some questions to ask.

Far down the street the Iceman calls 'Ice!—ICE!'

EPF [*stops and turns back to her*] About what?

SOPHIA. You!

EPF. What kind of questions?

SOPHIA. You don't know?

EPF. No! I don't know!

They size each other up.

ICEMAN [*nearer*] Ice!—ICE! . . . Ice!—ICE!

SOPHIA. Hm! [*Her eyes on Ephraim*] Hm!

ICEMAN [*as his cart trundles by*] Ice!—ICE! . . . Ice!—ICE!

EPF [*laughing suddenly*] That Iceman so WARM!—He don't know! He don't know! But the only kind of ICE I feeling for now is SNOW!

ICEMAN. Ice!—ICE!

EPF. Yer want a snowball, lady?

Sophia throws a piece of wet clothing at him. Ephraim laughs and drops the cloth back into the tub as Prince calls from the street.

PRINCE. Mavis! Mavis!

Prince comes running in along the alley-way. Ephraim starts off around the house to the shower. Prince and Ephraim exchange a greeting.

ICEMAN [*fading*] Ice!—ICE! . . . Ice!—ICE!

Prince is wearing a 'hot' shirt, gold-rimmed sun-glasses, American Air Force fatigue cap, shorts and loafers. A thick silver identification bracelet on one hand, a flashy black-faced gold wristwatch on the other. His shirt is unbuttoned, revealing bare skin. He is trailing a pair of swimming trunks.

MAVIS [*from her room*] Look me!—Look me! I here. Is you out there, Prince?

PRINCE. Who the hell else yer think it is? Come nah! Come nah! We ent have all day, yer know!

MAVIS. Awright! I gettin' meyself ready!

PRINCE. I have a taxi waiting out there, yer know.

MAVIS. Awright nah. I comin'.

PRINCE. God. These damn women. What they have to put on so—they always late. [*To Sophia*] Yer must excuse mey gettin' on so, neighbour—But I damn vex! I tell she I comin' nine o'clock—Is almost ten! She ent ready yet. MAVIS!

MAVIS. Ummmhmmmmmm! [*as if holding something in her mouth*].

PRINCE. Look like yer workin' hard today, neighbour?

Sophia puts down her washing and takes him in slowly.

SOPHIA. Mister! Yer ent have morning in yer mouth?

PRINCE. O Gord!—Sorry, sorry! [*He moves forward bowing low, one hand outstretched*] Mornin', neighbour. Mornin'!

SOPHIA. An' tell me this. An' yer livin' St. James?

PRINCE. That's right.

SOPHIA. An' how far St. James is from here?

PRINCE. 'Bout a mile.

SOPHIA. Well, how the hell I come your neighbour? My name is Mrs. Adams if yer didn't know. Yer get mey?

PRINCE. Awright, lady. I get yer. I get yer.

SOPHIA. An' I thank yer not to make so much damn noise when yer come in this yard. Yer get that too, mister?

PRINCE. I get yer, lady. Sorry. Sorry!

The taxi horn starts up. Prince shouts 'Awright'. And then he remembers Sophia's warning about noise. Instead of apologizing he tries to make conversation.

Look like allyer go have a good crop of mango when them trees start to bear. And is my kind of mango too. [*Fanning his shirt tail*] Wow! It makin' hot today, eh, neighbour?

Sophia looks up sharply.

. . . Mrs. Adams? . . . Neighbour?

Deadpans.

Mrs. Adams—I goin' an see what this damn girl doin'. Excuse mey, please—eh!

He gets to the steps as Mavis pulls the door open.

Jesus Christ marn!

MAVIS [*as she comes out*] Yer don't have to get on so jest

36

because yer takin' mey for a sea bath. Yer too damn showoff.
What the hell yer think it is at all!

She is dressed in a rather colourful two-piece sunsuit. Holding both her hands behind her she twists and wriggles as she tries to tie the straps of the upper half.

PRINCE. Yer better hush yer mouth, eh, girl! And come go.

MAVIS. Man, don't tell mey hush mey mouth, marn. I must talk. Here, tie that fer mey.

PRINCE. I thought yer say yer did ready. Now what the hell yer say yer have on here? Allyer sagger girls always on-dressing allyerself. Who is you? Rita Hayworth?

MAVIS. Tie it fer mey, nah! [*As he does so*] Yer getting on like a damn carterman, marn. Yer doesn't know that it don't matter where a woman goin'—She must always look she best.

PRINCE. I know when you look best to me, girl—Grrr!

He bares his teeth against her shoulder.

MAVIS. Stop that, nah! An' fix the thing fer mey!

PRINCE. I don't know wha' the hell yer makin' all this fuss for? Is only by the sea we goin'!

MAVIS. Star girls like me. . . .

PRINCE. Look. Hush yer mouth. An' come go!

MAVIS. But look how yer tie it. It still slack.

PRINCE [*striking her on the behind with his swim trunks*] So what! Go on, nah! Go on, nah! Sea water wastin'!

The taxi horn hoots again as they go off.

PRINCE: AWRIGHT!

SOPHIA. If it is the last thing I do—that little wiry bitch will have to leave this yard!

Inside Esther is singing 'Land of Hope and Glory'.

Esther!

ESTHER. Yes, Ma.

SOPHIA. Will yer hush yer mouth and let the baby sleep! . . . 'Lan' of Hope and Glory!

Mavis rushes back into the yard speaking to Prince who has remained outside in the taxi.

MAVIS. Don't worry to tell mey nothin' marn. Is you make me forget the damn bathin' suit! Come hurryin' mey an' confusin' mey. Yer say yer working nights at the Yankee PX. Daytime come so yer should want to sleep! Yer think I really want to go fer any damn sea bath!

As she hurries into her room and out again carrying the suit, Epf appears around the side of the house. Mavis pulls up. Mornin', doodoo!

EPF. Mornin'!

MAVIS. I see like *you* had yer bath!

EPF. Yer see nah.

MAVIS. I see. Not like some of we!

The taxi hoots.

I comin'! I comin'!

She disappears. And Sophia is left at boiling point.

SOPHIA. Dry lil' bitch! Yer want to tell me! A nasty little spoat like that have any right livin' among decent people?

The taxi is heard leaving.

EPF [*as he tosses the towel over the line*] Nothin' to do with me, lady.

SOPHIA. Nothin' to do with you! Allyer men! What the hell allyer care. The kind of thing that woman does carry on with here at night I shame to mention—far less fer Esther to see. All kinds of Yankee soldier and sailor in and out of the yard at night. An' that Prince!—I pray fer the day Charlie start working steady—so we could get out of all this.

EPF. To get out! That's the thing! Yer have to stay here— Living like this—Is as if yer trap!

SOPHIA. You so could talk!

EPF. Yes—I could talk! Look at that! [*He indicates the unfinished structure in the front yard*] All that waste. The blasted ole fool. He's got a house. Yet he starts putting that up. Three stories high. To live in!—Himself alone. Now is months since a workman was here. Don't you think Mrs. Adams—That instead of Ole Mack wastin' time and money on a thing like that!—Don't you think he could of build a

38

decent kitchen fer you? Fix up the bathroom?—Put on a roof? Use some paint back here? Not he. And I tell yer that girl shelling out to hold on to that room. The ole bastard!

Ephraim goes into his room.

SOPHIA [*suddenly switching the mood*] I think of him outside here in this yard last night, eh—An' I wish was you did come and ketch him. The ole reprobate. You should of seen him. Down on his knees. I couldn't help but laugh. I wonder if he really think that any nice young girl would want him? I wish yer did ketch him! [*And as Ephraim comes back to the door*] Tell me, nah? What was all that talk jest now about snow?

EPF. Snow? Yer askin' me mey business, lady. [*He smiles.*]

SOPHIA. Excuse me, sir. In future I will know my place.

And Charlie is heard singing as he comes in from the street.

CHARLIE'S VOICE. 'Comin' in on a wing and a prayer——"

SOPHIA. That damn loafer now comin' home!

CHARLIE'S VOICE. 'Comin' in on a wing and a prayer

Though there's one engine gone

We will still carry on

Comin' in on a wing and a prayer.'

Charlie appears, carrying a glass half full with Coca-Cola. He is a big bloated brown-skinned man. His clothes awry. The knot of his gaudy tie stuck crazily under the fold of the collar which is unbuttoned. A small Union Jack hangs from his jacket pocket. And perched on his head is a Royal Air Force officer's cap.

EPF. Like yer was havin' a time, Charlie.

CHARLIE [*almost falling down the steps*] You shudda been there! You shudda been there!

EPF [*rushing to his aid*] There where?

Ephraim takes the glass and helps Charlie to the bench.

CHARLIE. Princes Buildings. Reception last night for the troops that return. Buildings.—Jam cram. Flags. Coloured lights. Uniforms. Music. Dance! Freeness fer so! Everything free! Enough food and likka to choke a horse! And some of those boys touched glory! That black boy in blue! Squadron Leader Johnstone Guissippie—D.S.O., D.F.C. and bar! Black? Black like midnight! But talk about brave? Down twice. Bail out once! But up again—An' at them! [*He gets up*] This is his cap! And this? . . .

As he digs into his pocket, the Union Jack floats to the ground. He pulls out a pink Halloween nose with a thin moustache, holds it against his face.

Hitler's moustache!

Sophia comes down steps and confronts him. He bows to her.

Mornin', Mrs. Adams.

SOPHIA [*with quiet force*] Yer ent shame!

EPF. I see yer, Charlie. I got to take up duty.

Ephraim escapes to his room.
Charlie attempts to follow.

CHARLIE. Boy—Yer shudda been there!

ESTHER [*running out of the house into Charlie's arms*] Daddy, where were you?

CHARLIE. Mixing with heroes!

ESTHER. Heroes?

CHARLIE. Boys who was afraid—But did what they had to do.

SOPHIA. Yer finish yer needle work, Esther?

ESTHER. No, Ma.

SOPHIA. Then haul yerself inside and finish it.

Esther goes in.

CHARLIE [*looking at the coke in his hand*] I forgot the ice.

SOPHIA. Yer damn good fer nothing you! Comin' home drunk this time of mornin'!

EPF. You want some ice, Charlie?

CHARLIE. Good boy. Good boy. [*Goes in with Epf*] Boy—Yer shudda been there!

EPF. Next war, Charlie! Next war.

CHARLIE. Yer know—yer could a seen—yer could a seen how most of them boys was glad to be home. Most, yer know. Most. Glad to be . . . home!

And the masquerade is over.

40

EPH [*as he drops the ice into Charlie's glass*] Tough night, eh, Pa.

SOPHIA. Charlie! Charlie!

EPF. Yer want to rest a bit—yer could lay up in here.

Charlie sinks back gratefully on the bed.

SOPHIA. Charlie! . . . Charlie!

EPH [*coming out of the house*] Don't vex with him, Mrs. Adams. He must have had a hard night.

SOPHIA. All night long, Ephraim! To tell yer the truth—I don't want to vex—But is Esther I'm thinkin' about. If only Charlie would try a little harder. These next few weeks before school open so many things we find we have to buy. In them kind of schools yer can't go dress jest anyhow, yer know. All this Charlie know. But when the rum get in him so—pride—everything disappear. You wouldn't believe me, boy—But when I first knew Charlie he was spit and polish jest like you. Girls by the dozen. In them days he didn't have eyes for a body like me. But I went to every match he was playin' in. He was so handsome. Yer should have seen him.

EPH [*as he laces up his shoes*] When I was small—sometimes I'd listen to the old fellas talkin' cricket. And the things they used to say about that man. And that is what this country did to him.

SOPHIA. Not the country, Ephraim. A lot of others—with less chance than Charlie had—made the grade.

EPH. Them so had some special kind of privilege.

SOPHIA. Soon they makin' you inspector—what special privilege you have?

EPH. I may never know! . . . Trouble with Charlie—he was a dreamer. And ole as he is he ent loss that dream yet. But I'm young and I'm wide awake. And it ent my intention to remain here and grow a big white moustache like Ole Sam, who used to drive tramcar—and when the trolleys come— they pension him off with a pittance. This Trinidad has nothin' fer me! Nothin' I want!

SOPHIA. What about Rosa?

EPF. Rosa?

SOPHIA. Why all yer young men so?

EPF. So?

SOPHIA. Look—let me mind mey own business, yer hear. All-
yer young. Allyer could sort out allyer own salvation. I say
this fer yer though. You is a man with ambition!

EPF. I have mey plan!

*He picks up the Union Jack. There is a pause as she looks
at him—then she remarks flatly.*

SOPHIA. I hope it pointing in the right direction!—[*calling*]
Esther!

EPH. Don't worry for me, Mrs. Adams.

SOPHIA. Me!—Worry for you!—Not me!

EPH. That is what I mean.

He goes into his room.

SOPHIA. Hm! . . . Esther!

Going to the food safe she takes out some dried fish.

I think I do up some of this salt fish for your father.

She throws some into a dish and begins to strip it.

*Eph reappears at the door, cap in hand. As he comes down
the steps he puts on the cap.*

EPH. I'm off. Tell Rosa maybe i see her tonight. But I ent too
sure. The boys down at the depot throwing a party fer a fella
that going away.

He places the flag on the gate-post.

SOPHIA. What *this* one running from?

EPH. I'll ask him when I see him. I see yer.

SOPHIA. Run allyer! Run boys! Run! Sometimes I wish I
could do a little runnin' myself. They'd search hell to find
me. Esther!

ESTHER [*from inside*] Yes, Ma!

SOPHIA. Yer didn't hear mey calling yer?

ESTHER. No.

SOPHIA. Well, open yer ears when I want yer. I had to call yer
three times before yer answer. The baby wake?

ESTHER. No, Ma.

SOPHIA. He still sleepin'?

ESTHER. Yesss!

SOPHIA. Yer finish the needle work for Miss Jackman like I told yer?

ESTHER. Yes, Ma.

SOPHIA. Come and let mey see what yer do.

ESTHER. Awright, Ma.

SOPHIA. And don't keep mey here waitin' yer know. I have work to do. And I have no time to waste. Yer hear what I say, child?

Charlie is sitting up as Esther comes into the veranda—the needlework in her hand.

ESTHER. Look at it, Ma.

Sophia has been stripping the salt fish. She wipes her hands on her dress.

SOPHIA. Let me see.

ESTHER. O Gor, Ma! Yer will dirty it!

SOPHIA. Miss Fussy! Hand it here! . . . Esther! [*Esther hands over the needlework*] This is not the pattern Miss Jackman give yer to do!

ESTHER. No, Ma.

SOPHIA. Is a box yer want? Why yer like to have your own way so? Why yer can't do what people ask yer to do?

ESTHER. Ma!—this one was prettier. And . . . And it was much harder to do.

Sophia examines the work with a critical eye.

SOPHIA [*proudly*] Hm! Hm! . . . Charlie? Charlie [*Returning the cloth to Esther*] Here. Go on over. Show it to yer father.

And as Esther crosses Charlie comes down into the yard from Ephraim's room.

Charlie! Look at yer daughter's work. She's gettin' real smart with her fingers.

ESTHER. Look at it, Daddy.

Charlie takes the work from Esther. He holds it away from him at arm's length, blinking his eyes and nodding his head as he gazes at the cloth aglow with colour.

Yer like it?

CHARLIE. All those colours, Esther. Put so beautiful together.
  Sitting on the bench, Charlie puts an arm around Esther, pulling her close to him.
  One day, little girl—You going to be a star!
  Esther presses her body close, smiling at him. Sophia calls across the yard.

SOPHIA. Charlie!—Yer hungry?

CHARLIE [*without taking his eyes off the work*] Like a horse!

ESTHER. Can I have some, Ma. If is buljol yer makin'?

CHARLIE. All those colours. So beautiful together! So beautiful together!
  Rosa comes in from the street.

SOPHIA. You back awready. I have a message for yer. He say maybe he see yer tonight—But he wasn't too sure.

ESTHER. Rosa, what the police wanted?

ROSA. Well . . .
  As Rosa turns to Esther, she becomes aware of Charlie. Their eyes lock for a moment.
  It wasn't me they really wanted. . . . They . . .

JANETTE [*running in from the street*] You can't catch me. You can't catch me, Esther!

ESTHER. Oh, yes I can! Janette! Jerry!
  She runs out after Janette.

SOPHIA. Esther! Esther! That little girl, eh? All mornin' she been waitin' fer jest this chance. I don't know, nah. Is always me alone left to do everything. Nobody else don't seem to care.
  Rosa moves towards Charlie. She stands for a moment directly in front of him. And then turning away, she goes quickly into her room.

CHARLIE [*rising*] Sophie!—That girl look at me as though she'd seen a ghost!

SOPHIA. Go look in the mirror, mister—Then come tell me what yer see. [*Without rancour*] Charlie? All night? All morning?

44

CHARLIE. Not now, Sophie. Not now.

The children are calling.

CHILDREN. Hooop! Hooop! Yer can't catch me tho! Yer can't catch me tho! Yer can't catch me tho!

A VOICE. I caught yer! I caught yer! I—caught—yer!

Charlie is quite still. And Sophia is looking at him.

SOPHIA. Charlie—what's wrong?

CHARLIE. Nothin! [*Pulling himself together*] Nothing!

He goes back into Ephraim's room and sits on the bed. A solitary spot is left on Charlie as the lights go down.

A child chants: 'One, two, three, Mother catch a flea. Flea die. Mother cry—One, two, three! You to catch! You to catch! Hooop! Hooop!'

The children scream and laugh wildly as they play.

CURTAIN

Act Two

SCENE 1

Late that night. The sky is a silvery blue. Here and there a peeping star. The darkened houses look like ghosts in the flooding moonlight. The wind stirs in the trees and the galvanized roofing squeak and shudder. An owl hoots.

The mellow tones of a calypso drum can be heard. The music rising and falling as it rides the midnight air.

Mavis and an American soldier appear from the street and come down towards the yard. She is dressed in a thin, light green bodice, worn off the shoulders, and a full 'peasant type' skirt.

SOLDIER. Walla! Walla! Walla! I'm gonna walla in it. I gotta twenty-four-hour pass an' I'm gonna walla in it. Hey, come here! You gonna be good to me?

MAVIS. Yer have the right kind of money?

45

SOLDIER. I'm loaded. I gotta twenty-four-hour pass an' I'm loaded. [*Begins to paw.*]

MAVIS. Chut, man! Stop that. Come on, come inside.

She is about to enter her door when she stops suddenly— listening—looking over her shoulder towards the other side of the yard.

Wait for me a minute, Joe.

She pushes the soldier into her room.

She comes down the steps, picks up a stone. Pulling her arm back—she pitches the stone across the yard. It strikes against the shutters of the Adams' door. Immediately, the lights go on, the door is thrown open and Sophia appears in a long nightgown.

SOPHIA. Woman! Is the damn fool yer playin' nah?

MAVIS. Peeping, peeping, peeping! I wish the blasted stone did lick out yer eye!

SOPHIA. B'Jesus Christ! It would of been me an' you tonight! I would of rip yer to pieces like a mad dog—yer damn little whore!

MAVIS. Yer mother was the first one!

SOPHIA. And your mother before she!

The baby begins to cry.

Yer hear the baby how it crying? When the daytime come you ent have a blasted thing to do. . . .

MAVIS. Yer right! I does work too hard at night!

SOLDIER. Say!—Baby!—Lemme know—will yer? What the hell's going on here?

MAVIS. Come, Joe. Don't worry with she. Come inside.

They go in, closing the door.

SOPHIA. It ent me he have to worry with. An' if the Yankee would take my advice—he see the doctor first thing in the mornin'.

MAVIS [*comes rushing back into the yard*] Yer fat red bitch yer! I clean. I clean.

SOLDIER [*appearing at the door*] Do ya mean to tell me, Lady, this gal . . .

46

MAVIS. Come inside, Joe! Come inside. Don't worry with she!
*She grabs the American and pushes him into the room.
Then, turning back to Sophia*
Tomorrow mornin'! So help me God! I goin' down by the
Court house an' take out a summons fer yer. I will make
yer prove yer mouth before the doors of Court. What the
hell you know 'bout me?

SOLDIER [*reappearing*] I want to talk to her.

MAVIS. Always washing yer blasted mouth on people! Come,
Joe! Come! Don't worry with she!
*Mavis hustles him inside and bangs the door shut. Sophia
is left alone on the porch. The baby is crying.*

SOPHIA. Yer hear the baby, God? Yer hear him? No rest fer
me tonight! Grant mey patience—I asking yer! Save mey
from sinnin' mey soul!
*As the music from the victrola comes floating across the
yard, Sophia makes her final wish.*
And if it is the last thing yer do—show me a way to get that
little whore out of this yard! [*She goes inside.*]
*The sound of distant music, laughter and singing from a late
night party somewhere in the neighbourhood fades up and
mixes for a moment with the victrola music. These sounds fade
after a while—and only the sound of a lone guitar is heard.
And Ephraim's room is pushed forward so that it now dom-
inates the stage.*
*A match glows in the darkness of the room as Ephraim
lights a cigarette. Rosa is asleep on the bed. The shawl is
under her—part of it cascading to the floor. She is dressed in
a pale pink slip. Rosa stirs and opens her eyes.*

ROSA. Epf?
He takes a long drag on the cigarette, exhaling noisily.
Epf. Where you?

EPF. Here.
She rolls over on her back, groaning happily—luxuriously.

ROSA. I was sleeping. [*She smiles as she inquires languidly*] Who
was shoutin' so?

EPF. In the yard.

ROSA. Why they always have to quarrel so?

EPF. To ease the tension.

ROSA. What tension?

EPF. Of livin' like hogs!

Ephraim opens the shutters. Moonlight streams into the room.

ROSA. Umm! . . . Full moon tonight.

Epf, dragging on his cigarette, grunts a reply. There is a tenseness inside him. He exales without relaxing.

Epf—what's wrong?

EPF. Nothin'.

He leaves the window, goes over to the table and pours himself a drink. He drops some ice into the glass from the thermos.

Want some?

Rosa shakes her head.

Come on.

He holds the glass to her lips—she takes a tiny sip. The ear-rings are on the bureau. He takes them up. It is the pair from the first scene.

Nice ear-rings!

ROSA. Yer don't mind?

EPF. Yer want mey to?

ROSA. Yes.

EPF. Okay.

He throws the ear-rings back on to the bureau and taking the glass from her—drains it—ice and all.

ROSA [*sitting up*] Epf—what's wrong?

EPF. Nothin'.

ROSA. Yer so quiet tonight. An' these last few nights. . . .
Don't I please yer anymore?

EPF. Enough.

ROSA [*extends her hand to him*] Only enough?

Epf turns to look at her. He smiles.

EPF. Real Creole.

He sits on the floor beside the bed.

ROSA. Kiss me.

Epf puts two fingers to his lips and reaches out to touch her lips with his finger-tips. She takes his hand in hers, kissing it passionately. Then she pulls his hand down, placing it on her breast.

ROSA. Make love! [*Pause.*] Please!

Ephraim pulls his hand away slowly. He shakes his head.

Why?

EPF. Another time.

ROSA. Why?

He shrugs.

Why? . . . Awright. If yer don't feel [*Laughs*] Yer is a good-lookin' man—you know?

EPF. Good-looking. Like who?

ROSA. Robert Taylor.

EPF. Go 'way!

ROSA. James Stewart.

EPF. He good-looking?—Try again.

ROSA. William Holden. . . .

EPF. That's right—He an' me is twins.

ROSA. But look you!—Yer too fast with yer ugly self.

EPF. Jest now yer say I was handsome.

ROSA. That was jest now.

EPF. God!—Why all allyer woman so?

ROSA. Is we right.

EPF. Right?

ROSA. To tantalize.

EPF. Eh-heh?

They laugh.

An owl hoots. The owl hoots again.

ROSA. When owl hootin' so—somebody goin' to die.

Epf imitates the owl.

Don't!

Eph imitates the owl again.

She covers her ears and falls back on the bed.

Don't . . . don't!

49

Epf laughs—and kisses her on the cheek. They kiss. Her happiness is complete.

Off in the backyard next door someone calls to Ketch.

VOICE. Ketch!—Ketch!—Yer home?

KETCH. Yes, man. Wha' happening?

VOICE. Boy, I run all the way. Get yer guitar. Up Charlotte Street—Some Yankee at a party. Let we go an' sing a couple carriso—We pick up some money.

KETCH [*running up the street in the direction of the Voice*] I there with yer. Yer have a cigarette?

VOICE. No.

KETCH. Crise, man! Come go.

Ketch picks a happy tune on the guitar as they go. The guitar fades as they go off along the street.

EPF. We all after the Yankee dollar!

ROSA. When they goin' to make you inspector?

EPF. Don't know. Why?

ROSA. It would be nice.

EPF. I suppose.

ROSA. An' suppose one day—yer had a son. Wouldn't it be nice?—If yer was an inspector—instead of just an ole trolley-bus driver.

EPF. If ever I had a son, Rosa—I would never want him to feel shame fer his ole man. . . .

Getting up, he moves away to the window.

ROSA. And if yer had a daughter?

EPF. No different.

ROSA. I would like her to be born at the full of the moon. They say that if you're born at the full of the moon everything in yer life come plentiful and good.

EPF. Then we so must of been born last quarter.

They laugh together again.—A passing stroller on the road outside whistles 'When the lights go on again all over the world' as he goes along.

ROSA. [*quietly*] Ephraim?

She sits up.

50

EPF. Umm.

ROSA. Is Mr. Adams!

EPF. Mr. Adams?

ROSA. Is Mr. Adams break open the café.

EPF. . . . Charlie?

ROSA. Police found his hat under the counter by the cash register.

He looks at her unable to believe what he has heard.

They have it in the station, Epf. But they don't know yet whose own it is.

EPF. O Criiisssse!

The guitar has stopped and we hear the music from some distant steel band.

ROSA. I think Stephen know whose hat it is too.—But he wouldn't tell. He hate Mr. Mack too much. ∤. . . All night I been wanting to tell yer—O God, Ephraim! . . . Is my fault—that police found the hat. . . .

EPF. Your fault?

ROSA. It was the first thing I saw when I went in this mornin'. But I didn't know whose own it was until the police started questioning me about it.

EPF. Jesus Christ!

ROSA. Yer think they will find out?

EPF. What the hell else you think? A thousand times yer see Charlie with that hat. Allyer women ent have no sense! Christ!—Not Charlie!—Anybody else!—Not Charlie!

He hurries out into the yard and on to Sophia's porch. He stands there for a moment as though wanting to call someone before turning and rushing back to his room.

. . . Earlier tonight—You and me—We talk about this thing. We even mention Charlie—Joking at how he come in drunk this mornin'—AND THEN YER LAY DOWN THERE!—AND NOT ONE SINGLE WORD YER SAY ! !

ROSA. I didn't know how to tell yer, Ephraim.

EPF. ALL ALLYER WOMAN LIVIN' FOR ONE THING !

Rosa. Don't blame me, Ephraim!

Epf. Don't blame you! You so damn hot to ring up police for seventy dollars Ole Mack could well afford to lose! Yer think Esther and Mrs. Adams could afford to have Charlie in jail?

Rosa. But the police. . . .

Epf. Police my arse! Look at them ear-rings!—An' this chain! Old Mack givin' yer all this fer nothin'? The fancy clothes! —wristwatch!—and nice shoes yer wearing!—How yer come by them?

Rosa. Epf?

Epf. I young and I strong. An' that is all you want with me. Even up to this last minute gone—I wasn't sure in mey mind. I say things work out for me—I SEND FER YER! But from now on, girl—Yer sweet ole man alone will have to do. . . . Look at these! Look at these! Yer see?

He has gone to the trunk which he opens.

Yer see these? Passport! Ticket! Them few travellers' checks! Yer know what that for? Tomorrow night—This time so! I gone! Four thousand miles across the sea!—To Liverpool!

Rosa [*bewildered*] Liver-pool?

Epf. Yer think I stay here to come like Charlie?

Rosa. Charlie?

Epf. Sweet-mouth Charlie! Stinkin' in jail next week!

Rosa. Ephraim—yer can't go.

Epf. Only if that tanker change the schedule!—I wouldn't be going!

Rosa. I'm pregnant.

There is a pause.

Epf. Pregnant?

Rosa. Yes.

Epf. Fer who?

Rosa [*smiling*] Epf!

Epf. This is no joke.

Rosa. Fer you.

Epf. Make me laugh.

ROSA. Fer you, Ephraim.

EPF. Trap.

ROSA. No.

EPF [*wildly*] TRAP! Who the hell yer think yer talkin' to? TRAP!! Go tell yer ole man that!

Mavis's voice as she pounds the partition wall.

MAVIS. Ay!—Allyer! People want to sleep, yer know!

EPF [*rushing out of his room to pound on Mavis's door*] Enough of that you!

MAVIS [*voice*] O Gor, doodoo-darlin'!—Yer HOT tonight!

Ephraim storms down into the yard. Somewhere in the distance we hear the rhythmic pounding of a steel band. Inside Rosa lies across the bed, crying. After a moment Ephraim goes back into the room.

EPF. Rosa. Rose. Rose—Don't shed no tears for me—I was never worth that kind of water. Rosa—Listen to me! Look! Look!

He has taken a framed photograph from his trunk. Kneeling beside the girl he pulls her to him.

Yer see this picture of ole Grandma here? . . . She took care of me from the time I small—till I grow a man! My ole man died when I was five years old. When I was six—my mother pick up with another man—went off to Curacao! —and left me flat! For nearly a whole week I went hungry— till Grandma came and found me and took me home with her. So it was only me and Gram from all that time. . . . Then come a time. I began to make my plans. I find that she was in my way. I wanted to save money!—But she was in my way. So one day—I went to her—Told her—I was putting her in the poor house . . . Four days!—After I took her there—she died.

ROSA [*makes the sign of the cross*] O God!

He has told his story without any display of emotion.

EPF. When they knew she was dying. They send and call me. She was lying there on the bed. I couldn't believe it was she. In four days—she had sort of—wasted away. I stood up by

the door—I couldn't go no farther. She was looking at me.
But I just stood there. Shame! eating me! . . . I heard her
ask the nurse for me to come near. Perhaps—to forgive me
—I don't know. But I couldn't go. I couldn't go. Then she
told the nurse: Tell that boy if he can't come nearer—he
might as well go! . . . She died that night.

ROSA. Eph!

She moves to console him.

EPF [*pulling away*] DON'T TOUCH ME! So don't think—
Don't think a little trap like you could ketch me—just by
sayin' yer going to have a baby fer mey. When that boat
whistle blow!—It mean I leaving all this behind! This
picture!

He throws the frame spinning to the floor.

You and Ole Mack! Charlie! Mrs. Adams! Esther!—The
whole damn blasted lot!

ROSA. No.

EPF. Listen to me, Rosa! I got a life to live! Awright! So I stay
here. I come an inspector on the trolley. To what end? Turn
macco like the rest. Stand at a bus stop. Hop on the trolley.
Check the tickets. Hop off the trolley! To what end, Rosa?
Just so as to see the conductors don't rob the blasted City
Corporation?

ROSA. EPHRAIM!

EPF. That is not for me! Outside somewhere in the world I
feel for certain sure it got more for me than that!

ROSA [*she moves towards him*] What about me?

EPF. You?

ROSA. The baby?

EPF. Don't bring that damn nonsense to me. I'm a big man.
Not no damn little boy. Ready to get myself tie-up the
minute some woman tell me she makin' child. So if that is the
plan yer hatch to ketch me—This is one big boy that sorry.
That plan ent go work at all.

ROSA. Yer not going to marry me?

EPF. Here. Look yer dress. Put it on and go 'bout yer business.

He throws the dress at her, and pushes her towards the door.
Crying out, Rosa turns beating at him with her fists.

ROSA. Yer is a damn worthless nigger! Yer mother walk out on you! You kill yer own grandmother! . . .

Ephraim lifts her off the ground and literally throws the girl out of his room, hurling her dress, shoes and the shawl after her.
Do you think!—Do you think I want a man like you to marry me or to father my child? You go!—You go wherever the hell yer want to go! And when the time come so for yer to dead—I hope yer dead like the bastard you are—Yer two foot stick up high in the air!

EPF. Thanks! An' if that is all yer have to say fer good-byes! Good-bye!

Slamming the door shut, he returns inside. Rosa is left alone in the yard.

The guitar strums. The Singer's voice wails 'Blueslike'—a taunting calypso refrain.

VOICE. 'Brown skin gal stay home and mind baby
Brown skin gal stay home and mind baby
I'm goin' away in a sailin' boat—
And if I don't come back
Throw 'way the damn baby. . . .

The Singer's voice begins to fade. Ephraim picks up the photograph as—

THE LIGHTS GO DOWN

Act Two

SCENE 2

The next morning. The sky is overcast. The light less brilliant. A lone calypso drum plays in the distance.
Rosa is in the veranda. She is barefoot—still in her slip. She stands awkwardly. Her arms around the veranda post—her head

and belly pressing against it. One foot drawn up against the ankle of the other.

Sophia's washing, a riot of colour, blocks out the view to the street—the line bellying with the weight of damp clothing. She has left a path just wide enough to allow a passage through to the gate.

Suddenly from inside—Sophia begins to shout.

SOPHIA. Charlie, get up man, get up. Time yer get out of the house and do some work, yer know. Yer lay down in the bed this mornin' till sun burn yer behind—before yer get up. Yer had yer breakfast. Almost lunch-time now—Yer sit down in a chair to sleep. Here—Take the bats and the glue and the gimlet and everything. Go outside. Go, go, go!

Charlie shuffles through the door with several cricket bats tucked under his arm. One bat is quite new and recently oiled. In his tool kit is stacked all the paraphernalia of the bat-mender's trade—knife, ball of white twine, mallet, linseed oil, etc.

Shamefaced—he walks past Rosa, down the steps and crosses the yard towards the bench. He sets his tool kit on the ground, the bats against the wall of Ephraim's room, and sitting down, begins to work.

Rosa's eyes are on him.

SOPHIA. And young Mr. Murray wants his bats this afternoon.

CHARLIE. He'll get them.

SOPHIA. [*coming on to the porch*] Wonders will never cease! . . . Ay-ay!—Rosa? You still here? I thought you had gone . . . Rosa, child—What's wrong? . . . out here in yer slip like that.

Rosa makes a funny movement with her head.

Rosa . . . yer told him?

ROSA. Yes.

SOPHIA. Last night?

ROSA. Yes.

SOPHIA. Come—Yer can't stop out here like this. Come, go inside. I hot up some coffee. It won't take long.

Rosa goes in. The music fades.

Esther comes in from the street singing a play song—'Tante siroup c'est doux, Madelina'. She has tied Charlie's Union Jack about her head as if it were a bandana.

Esther!—An' yer were out in the road?

ESTHER. Yes, Ma.

SOPHIA. Is flag pole yer playin' or what? Take that damn stupid thing off yer head and go tell Stephen in the café that Rosa ent comin' out this morning.

ESTHER. Awright, Ma.

Esther takes the flag from her head as she goes out. Sophia crosses to light in stove.

SOPHIA. That Ephraim! If he was here—I give him a RED hot piece of mey mind.

Prince comes quietly in from the street, ducks under the clothes-line and calls softly: 'Mavis'. . . .

Now what the devil wrong with this stove this morning—it wouldn't light!

PRINCE. Good mornin', Miss Lady. Mavis there?

SOPHIA. To hell with you!

PRINCE [*pulling up*] Ay-ay! Look mey trouble.

He sucks his teeth.

That is what man does get fer playing gentleman—Mavis! Mavis!

He bangs on the door.

Mavis! . . What do this girl?—She must be dead—She can't hear. Mister—Excuse me. You know whether that girl inside?

CHARLIE. I don't, son.

PRINCE. Mavis!

SOPHIA [*shouting*] Look!—You! Go some other blasted place and make yer noise!

PRINCE [*shouting back*] Lady—I callin' mey woman!—awright!

He turns and pounds on the door.

Mavis?

MAVIS [*sleepily*] One minute.

PRINCE. Come nah, come nah! Open the door.

MAVIS. Prince, yer can't come in.

PRINCE. How yer mean—I can't come in?

MAVIS. I restin'.

PRINCE. Look!—Don't tell mey no damn foolishness nah, girl. Open the door.

MAVIS. Oh Gor!—Prince. I sleepin'.

PRINCE. Sleepin'? This time of mornin'! [*To Sophia*] Lady, you ever hear that?

Sophia laughs with him and then repeats the word 'Sleepin'!' Prince turns away and the smile is gone from his face as he calls to Mavis.

AWRIGHT! Who the hell yer think yer foolin'? Who yer have in there?

MAVIS. No-bor-dee!

PRINCE. Then open the door! Open the door!

He waits a moment.

Open the door yes girl—or yer want me to break it down?

MAVIS. Awright then. I comin'.

A bolt is thrown from inside. The door opens slowly— tentatively.

Look mey.

PRINCE. Move aside you!

He pushes her into the yard.

Who the hell yer hidin' in there!

He is half-way through the door.

Oho! So is so! A pink face Yankee soldier boy! The fellas tell me yer layin' up with Yankee. I say they lie. Come, Joe! Come an' get me!

He backs out into the yard.

SOLDIER [*coming to the door*] Take it easy, buster. That gal brought me here last night!

PRINCE. No other man touch my woman, marn. Come—an' get mey, Joe.

SOLDIER. I don't want no trouble, buster.

PRINCE. I know! All allyer Yankee yellow!

He charges head-first at the soldier—they crash into Mavis's room.

MAVIS [*rushing into the fray*] O God! Prince, the Yankee goin' kill yer! Don't hit him! Don't hit him! Yer can't fight, Prince, yer know yer can't fight.

She runs out into the yard.

He can't fight. Ever since yer had yer hernia yer can't fight. Don't hit him! Don't hit him!

She runs back into the room and then out again into the yard, her hand to her head.

She takes her hand away from her head. And there is blood on it. Her eyes bulge at the sight of the blood. She screams and bolts out of the yard, through the gate and out towards the street, shouting:

Murder! Murder! POLICE! MURDER!

PRINCE. Mavis! Mavis!

He comes rushing out of the room and races after her, ducking just in time to avoid running into the line.

Charlie laughs uproariously. The American comes out and walks slowly towards the gate. The soldier stops and turns to Charlie.

SOLDIER. It ain't much fun, Pop, when you gotta fight the men for it!

The soldier goes out.

SOPHIA. Some of these Yankees ent have no shame! You—yer right to laugh. All allyer men just the same. No peace—No peace at all in this yard—but that don't worry you. Let us all wallow—happy in this nastiness.

Charlie begins to whistle.

Yes! Go on! Whistle. Pretend it ent you I talkin' to. If yer wasn't the kind of man yer is we long been out of this. With a nice little house and garden—All we own—up Laventille. And a drawing-room where Esther could entertain her little friends. I shame to have her bring anybody here. Yer think you does think 'bout she. Put in the application! Put in the application! Day after day I tellin' yer. But not you. You had to be the last—with thousands before yer!

CHARLIE. I didn't know you couldn't of write.

SOPHIA. Application fer house and thing like that is man business.

CHARLIE. I see.

SOPHIA. Late!

Esther returns.

ESTHER. Ma—I gave Stephen the message.

SOPHIA. Thanks, darling!

JANETTE. Cooo-ooo!

ESTHER. Coooo-ooo!

JANETTE. Are you ready?

ESTHER. Coming. I goin' now—eh, Ma?

SOPHIA. Awright, darling. Enjoy yerself. But see and come back here in time. Three o'clock is late enough. Yer hear mey?

ESTHER. Yes, Ma.

JANETTE. Come on, Esther, I've got the sandwiches. We're late. The Rebeiros are waiting.

ESTHER. G'bye, Daddy!—Going, Ma!

Epf ducks under the line and playfully blocks Esther's path.

EPF. Hey, Esther. Where yer goin'?

ESTHER. We're going on a ramble up the hills.

And she skilfully dodges past him and runs laughing towards the street.

Ephraim comes in carrying a shopping bag. A second-hand sailor's pea-jacket is stuffed into it. He hurries up the steps to his room.

CHARLIE. Hey, Epf!

EPF. Hey, Charlie! . . . Looks like yer got him down to it, Mrs. Adams.

Sophia ignores this remark and goes into Rosa's room.
The lady like she out of humour this morning.

CHARLIE. Yer know how she is sometimes. Boy, look—I show yer this.

He reaches for one of the bats.

Look at this bat, boy—and he's been using it most of the season!

Epf has put down the shopping bag and has come back into the yard to examine the bat. He wants to go about his business —but he forces himself to stay.

EPF. Whose own?

CHARLIE. Young Murray.

EPF. Royal College?

CHARLIE. That's right. Look at the face of that bat, Epf. Hardly an edge. An' he been using it most of this season. Epf! Young Murray is going to be one of the real big ones in a couple of years!

EPF. Yea.

CHARLIE. He's goin' be a useful little bowler too, yer know.

EPF. The selectors plannin' big things fer him, I hear.

CHARLIE. Yes. But they should ease him. He's kind of young, yer know. Try to break them in too early sometimes. And they get break fer good. That new one over there is his as well. Gets new bats by the dozen, that boy. His ole man holding a lot of dough.

EPF. Yes. So I hear.

CHARLIE. In my day, Epf—I use to get my bats second-hand. An' sometimes they had to last me from season to season. But my big talent was with the ball. I used to trundle down to that wicket—an' send them down red hot! They don't make them that fast these days. The boys don't keep in condition. Today they send down a couple of overs—they are on their knees. But in my time, John, Old Constantine, Francis, them fellas was fast! Fast! Up in England them so help put the Indies on the map.

EPF. I only saw you once on the green, Charlie. Yer was kind of past yer prime. But the ole brain was there! And batsmen was seein' trouble! Trouble, man! And I say this to you now, papa—You was class!

CHARLIE [*laughing as he warms to old memories*] Ever hear

about that time when I knocked ole Archie Seagram's bails back fifty yards from the wicket?

Epf laughs sympathetically.

EPF [*leaning on the bat*] Charlie . . . What was the plan?

CHARLIE [*startled*] Plan?

EPF. Your dream!

CHARLIE. It was something more real than a dream that went from me.

EPF. What?

CHARLIE [*smiles*] Boy—I was pushing thirty. Hard. Strong as a bull—and at the height of mey power as a bowler. None better, boy. Nowhere—None better. Ask the ole timers— they tell you. But for the West Indian tour to England that year—I didn't even get an invite to the trials.

EPF. Why, Charlie?

CHARLIE. In them days, boy—The Savannah Club crowd was running most everything. People like me either had to lump it or leave it.

EPF. It ent much different now, Charlie.

CHARLIE. Is different—A whole lot different. In them times so when we went Barbados or Jamaica to play cricket they used to treat us like hogs, boy. When we went on tours they put we in any ole kind of boarding-house. The best hotels was fer them and the half-scald members of the team—So in Twenty-seven when we was on tour in Jamaica I cause a stink, boy. I had had enough of them dirty little boarding-house rooms. I said either they treat me decent or they send me back. The stink I made got into the newspapers. They didn't send me back. But that was the last intercolony series I ever play. They broke me, boy.

EPF [*quietly*] Fer that?

CHARLIE. I should of known mey place. If I had known mey place, Epf, I'd a made the team to England the following year. And in them days, boy—the English County clubs was outbidding each other fer bowlers like me. But the Big Ones here strangled my future, boy.

EPF. Just like that.

CHARLIE. Like that.

EPF. Jesus Christ!

CHARLIE. Don't heat yerself up. All that is—long ago. And is possible perhaps that some men wasn't born to make it.

EPF [*bitterly*] This country, Charlie? Jesus Christ! To think that a man who could of play class cricket like you.

CHARLIE. Boy—There were other things. Little things. Big things. Altogether pushing yer out of the stream—and on to the bank—So that yer rot slow in the sun. . . . You don't know yet, boy—what life is like—when things start to slide from under yer.

Sophia comes into the veranda from Rosa's room. She glances scornfully at the two men.

SOPHIA. Ephraim! Yer ent have nothin' better to do than to keep Charlie outside here talkin'?

CHARLIE. Is awright, Sophie. Is jest a little ole talk.

SOPHIA. A li'l ole work is what I want to see. [*To Ephraim*] An' I want to have a word with *you*!

MAVIS [*from the street*] Pampam-palam! Pampam-palam.

It is the wedding march toned up to calypso beat.

CHARLIE. Fire ram de fe!

SOPHIA. A bucket of water would soon cool she!

Mavis comes in—a Johnson's band-aid under one eye, and displaying a ring on her left hand. Prince follows some distance behind looking sheepish. Mavis is chanting the wedding march. It is toned up to calypso beat.

MAVIS. Ay allyer! Look! Look! Look! Mey man put a ring on mey finger. He say he go make a respectable women out of mey. Hayhahyai! It got a lot of them will give they left hand fer a ring like this.

PRINCE. Hush yer mouth, nah girl. Hush nah.

MAVIS. No. Let mey show them. It got a lot of them what playin' they high and mighty—'cause they have ring on they finger. They don't talk to people like me. So let mey show them. Ay! You! Look!—Look at mey left hand. Yer see?

63

Mrs. Prince I have be call from now on. Princess Mavis. That's me.

PRINCE. Come, come!—Come inside nah! The world don't have to know.

MAVIS. I tellin' it jest the same! Pampampalam! Pampampalam!—Pampampalam—pampalm—pampalm!

Prancing and gyrating, she moves towards Ephraim.

That going be wedding! And don't think every Tom, Dick and Mary goin' get invite. Allyer could wait fer that! Epf doodoo! You could come!

Throwing her arms around him she kisses him full on the mouth.

. . . Mr. Adams, you want to come? Come too!

As she turns towards Charlie, Prince moves in to her.

PRINCE. Come you, come inside. Your makin' a damn fool of yerself. And from now on none of this Yankee stupidness.

They disappear inside.

SOPHIA. Bitch!

She goes into Rosa's room with a cup of coffee.

CHARLIE. Sophie! . . . Can we two men have a li'l coffee?

SOPHIA [*from inside*] Take it!

CHARLIE [*going up the steps to get the coffee*] Boy—they had some of them like Mavis out by the Buildings Monday night. Yer should of seen them guzzle the free likka that was flowin'. Them women! [*He laughs.*] But, boy! It was great! Great! The boys in their campaign ribbons. Normandie—Libya—Italy—all over the place. And last Monday night it was a hero of a welcome for everyone of them.

EPF [*abruptly*] Charlie—I got to go.

CHARLIE. Have some coffee, man.

EPF. Thanks. But I got somethin' I got to pick up.

CHARLIE. See yer later then, boy.

EPF. See yer, Charlie.

Ephraim puts down the bat and crosses the yard towards the gate. Old Mack ducks under the clothes-line. Charlie comes down the steps.

OLD MACK. Well, young man. How are things with you?

EPF. Never better.

He pushes past Old Mack and goes out. The old man turns to look at Ephraim as he goes through the gate.

CHARLIE. Some coffee, Mr. Mack?

OLD MACK. No thanks, Charlie.

CHARLIE. I got a whole pot going.

OLD MACK. Never in the daytime.

CHARLIE. Gimme a cup—any time.

He crosses towards his workbox.

OLD MACK. Is—Rosa—in?

Recalling the undignified way he left the yard on his last visit Old Mack plays it cautious—for certainly Mrs. Adams must have told everyone an exaggerated version of the incident.

CHARLIE [*absently*] Ummm?

OLD MACK. Rosa. Is she—in?

CHARLIE. Oh!—Yes! Yes! My wife's in there with her.

OLD MACK. I heard she wasn't feeling very well.

CHARLIE. Yes. My wife sent Esther a little while ago with a message to Stephen.

He sits down.

OLD MACK. I wonder if there is anything I can do?

He moves towards veranda steps.

Rosa? Rosa?

SOPHIA [*from inside Rosa's room*] She'll be out in a minute.

OLD MACK [*going up steps and into veranda*] I thought she was ill! Stephen said she sent a message saying she was ill.

He is at the door.

SOPHIA [*coming to door*] Yes. But hearing you out there—she feel better awready.

OLD MACK. Mrs. Adams—I only came to find out if there was anything I could do to help.

SOPHIA. Now yer know!

She slams the door.

Controlling his anger, he turns and comes back down the steps towards Charlie who is busily at work on a bat. Old Mack watches Charlie for a while. And then to get over the embarrassment of being made to stand out in the yard and wait, he starts up a conversation with Charlie.

OLD MACK. Well, Charlie—how are things with you?

CHARLIE. Flourishing, flourishing! Got too many as it is.

OLD MACK. Good!

Now Charlie looks up—but he does not look at Old Mack.

CHARLIE. Things keep on the way they going—the next few months should see me right. And now that the little girl win scholarship to High School—I want more than ever to keep things going.

OLD MACK. It'll keep. Things start to go for you—they'll keep. You heard about my bit of misfortune, of course?

CHARLIE [*back at work*] Yes. I heard.

OLD MACK. Seventy dollars! Gone! Just like that! Bastards! I get my hands on them!—Old as I am, Charlie—I'd show them a thing or two! Break into my café! Smash my register! And as to our smart police! Yesterday they are crawling all over the place. And what you think they find?—A hat!

CHARLIE. Hat?

He blinks—and jerks his head away—trying to remember.

OLD MACK. You know one thing I'm certain sure of, Charlie? That boy Stephen—who runs the café for me—he knows something. But I know—he'd never tell. Charlie—yer take a boy off the street. Yer treat him as if he was your own. Yer trust him. Yer put him in charge of a café. Yer think he grateful. That boy hates me, Charlie. Hates me so he'd even rob me. Is hard.

CHARLIE. That's life!

Sophia has come into the veranda and catches the end of Old Mack's talk with Charlie.

SOPHIA. Is hard—because allyer so too blasted bad.

A chorus of raucous laughter comes from Mavis's room.

She so over there good fer you.

PRINCE [*from inside*] Le' we go, girl.

MAVIS. I comin'. But I tellin' yer from now. I don't want no damn coolie talcurry. We goin' to a Chinee restaurant. [*As she comes down into the yard*] Ay-ay—Ole Mack! Yer hear I engage? That woman there tell yer, nah? [*Pointing at Prince*] That is the man.

PRINCE. Come go, nah, girl. Come go.

And as Rosa comes into the veranda

MAVIS [*maliciously*] Ay! always get the ring first. Then get the baby. [*And as they go*] Good afternoon, Mrs. Adams.

SOPHIA. Keep yer damn fastness for yer friends.

Mavis laughs as she goes out with Prince.

Mr. Mack—right to yer face I telling you again! Yer should be ashame! Ashame! Lettin' that woman live here among decent people!

OLD MACK. She pays her rent, Mrs. Adams.

SOPHIA [*scornfully*] And that is all you care.

OLD MACK. Not quite. She always pays on time. Get me as reliable a tenant, Mrs. Adams. I give her notice tomorrow.

Ephraim, carrying an empty holdall, comes in along the alley-way as Old Mack moves towards Rosa. Ephraim stops at the gate.

Rosa? Anything I can do? Stephen told me that you were ill and that you weren't coming out today.

ROSA. Yes—but I'm feeling all right now.

OLD MACK. Good. Good. I've got the car outside. I'll give you a drop.

ROSA. Thank you.

Epf stands blocking the path through the gate. He makes no attempt to step aside. Epf's eyes are on Rosa. There is a tight pause.

OLD MACK. Young man . . . If yer don't mind . . . we'd like to pass.

Another pause. Then Ephraim steps aside. Old Mack and Rosa go out. Epf crosses towards his room.

OLD MACK [*as they go out*] From now on, Rosa—when you are there in the café—I want you to keep a sharp eye on things. That boy Stephen—It isn't right, Rosa. I took that boy off the street. Gave him a job. Tried to make him respectable and I'm telling you, Rosa. . . .

SOPHIA. And you call yerself a man!

EPF. Mrs. Adams—leave it, nah.

He disappears inside, slamming the door as Sophia crosses towards him. Sophia wants to go after him but changing her mind, she addresses Charlie.

SOPHIA. Charlie. I want yer to do something fer me. Fer really right now I don't trust meyself. Yer know what that boy's been planning all these months? [*And suddenly exasperated*] Charlie! Yer don't hear mey talkin' to yer?

But there is no answer. No movement from Charlie.

Charlie. Charlie—something wrong?

CHARLIE. Sophie!

SOPHIA. Yes.

CHARLIE. Sophie!—I have to give myself up!

SOPHIA. Give yerself up?

CHARLIE. He suspect is Stephen.

SOPHIA. He?—Suspect who? God knows I ent know what yer talkin' about! Who Stephen? Stephen in the café? . . . O God! O God! . . . Charlie!—What possess yer? . . . What . . . Possess yer . . . Charlie? . . .

CHARLIE. Was . . . for Esther . . . for school. . . .

SOPHIA. No—Charlie! . . . No!

CHARLIE [*taking a roll of bills from his shirt pocket*] Don't cry, Sophie . . . Most of the money still here . . . I'll give it back.

SOPHIA [*comes down the steps*] But—Monday night, Charlie . . . You was in the Buildings.

CHARLIE. No. I was outside there for a while. I didn't go in. Yer had to have a ticket to go in. I left there about one o'clock to come home. When I got by the café—like something took hold of me. After that I went back to the Buildings. Some of the people had gone home. And they was lettin' in a few stragglers. I got in. I join some fellas at the bar and drank 'til mornin'. O God! . . . Forgive me,

Sophie. I bring shame on allyer. On you. An' Esther. An' the baby.

Sophia comforts him. Her arms around him.

SOPHIA. Hush, boy! Hush! Don't cry! Don't cry!

CHARLIE. It didn't seem like real stealing . . . somehow . . . Taking it from Ole Mack.

SOPHIA. I know, Charlie. I know. Twelve-fifty a month he takes from we—fer that stinking little room! It couldn't be stealin'. It couldn't be. Hush now, boy! Hush! Hush! Sophie will find a way. The money? I'll take and give to Rosa. Ask her to give it to Ole Mack. Ask her to talk to him for Esther and the little baby sake. He'll listen to Rosa. I sure he'll listen. He *have* to listen. . . Hush! Hush, boy!

Ephraim comes down the steps.

EPF. Mrs. Adams? . . . Let me have that money! Let me have it! Ole Mack will take it! He'll take it, Mrs. Adams—or so help me, God! I'll ram it down his throat!

The young policeman appears along the alley-way as Sophia reaches for the money in Charlie's pocket. But now Ephraim's attention is riveted on the policeman as the young man pauses for a moment at the gate. The Lights go down.

CURTAIN

Act Three

SCENE 1

It is now the middle of the afternoon. The sky is still overcast. The atmosphere heavy with moisture. Only a few pieces of clothes remain hanging on the line.

'Ice! Ice!' The Iceman calls as his cart trundles by. 'Ice! Ice!'

Prince is sitting on the step—sipping a beer. Mavis stands above him at her door. She has a bowl of rice in her hand. She picks at the rice in the bowl, throwing the broken and discoloured

bits into the yard. Ephraim is in his room. He has been drinking.
A flask of Vat 19 is on the bureau.

MAVIS. Prince, boy. To tell the truth—I sorry fer Mr. Adams.
I always did like him, yer know. He never trouble with a
soul. But as to that Lady Adams and she precious little girl
child! I wouldn't give a damn if was either one of them!
Yer think they jail him?

PRINCE. How I to know?

MAVIS. Yer should of see the lady. She left here about an hour
ago. Dress-up in she Sunday best. She look like a Christmas
tree! Goin' to try an' borrow to bail him out, I suppose.
High mind!—but low behind!

PRINCE [*rising, tries to change the subject*] Come go fer a sea-
bath? I know a fella would lend me a pick-up truck.

MAVIS. Sea-bath? Where? Move aside. Let me pass.

She comes down the steps, and crosses to the gate. She
stands looking out along the alleyway.

PRINCE. Carenage. Maracas. Anywhere.

MAVIS. Nah. I don't feel so, nah, boy. The sun not shining.

PRINCE. Come go, nah. It making kind of close.

MAVIS. Eh-eh! Not today. Today I staying right here so as to
find out all what happen. That woman always was minding
mey business. She bawl like a pig, I hear, when the police
come and take him.

Prince sits again. Outside in the street Esther calls to her
friend. Ephraim pours a drink.

ESTHER. Bye, Jan! See you later! Bye.

JANETTE. Bye!

MAVIS [*running back to Prince*] The child like she come back.

ESTHER [*as she comes in*] Ma!—Daddy!—I'm back!—And is
not three o'clock yet.

MAVIS. Ma!—Daddy!—I'm back!—Ma-ah!

PRINCE [*to Mavis*] Hush yer mouth!

ESTHER. Ma-ah!

She goes into the house.

PRINCE. Wha' happen to yer? Yer ent have no feelin's? Is only a little girl.

MAVIS. Get you! Not me, boy. I have no time fer mock sentiment. She mother struttin' 'bout the yard like she was Queen of Sheba ... And, boy, you hear what I hear? I hear she trap Mr. Adams.

PRINCE. How you mean, 'trap'?

MAVIS. That little girl ent even Mr. Adams's child.

PRINCE. Where the hell you get that?

MAVIS. Since they arrest him, everybody talkin'!

PRINCE. Mavis!—yer know something?

She waits for it.

In all the time I know you—I never realize yer so blasted ignorant!

MAVIS. Take me or leave me!—I just as how yer find me!

And turning away Mavis moves towards the water tap.

PRINCE. I have a damn good mind to come there and ...

MAVIS. Yer see this? Yer see this? [*Holding out the hand with the ring*] Don't think yer goin' hit me as yer damn well like now that I have this, yer know. I will make yer sorry, boy! Sorry! We ent married yet, yer know!

Ephraim comes to the door, an empty cigarette packet in his hand.

EPF. Hey, fella! Gimme a cigarette.

PRINCE. A cig—sure, sure.

He offers a pack of American cigarettes.

EPF. I'm dry.

PRINCE. Help yerself—Take the lot!—It got a lot more where that come from.

EPF. Thanks.

PRINCE. My pleasure, pal.

MAVIS [*handing the bowl of rice to Prince as she crosses to Ephraim*] Ay-ay!—Doodoo, darlin'! I didn't know you was inside. I say you was out helpin' to bail out somebody.

EPF. Bail out who?—You?

MAVIS [*throwing her arms around him*] O God, boy! I *like* yer so!

71

EPF. Ay, Prince. Yer want a job driving trolley?

PRINCE. Me! Not me, Joe! I doing too well with the Yankee!

He has crossed to the porch. He puts down the bowl of rice, picks up a cricket bat and advances menacingly towards Mavis. Mavis is too taken with Ephraim to notice the action.

MAVIS. Tell me, nah. Tonight. Is leave—yer leaving she fer true? Is true yer goin' England? Boy! Last night! Allyer two! O God! . . . You was *my* man!—Yer never to treat *me* so!

EPF [*speaking to Prince as he eases himself out of Mavis's embrace*] I see yer.

MAVIS. Anytime! Right now—if yer like! So tonight—*if* yer go!—I sure it will bring yer back!

Her eyes follow Ephraim as he goes into his room. Then she turns to Prince and teases him with a small gesture of her body. He nice, eh?

PRINCE. Always making a damn fool of yerself!

MAVIS. Ah—Go way you! Yer just *jealous*!

But for her the teasing is over. She crosses to the porch, picks up the bowl and starts towards her room.

I goin' an' cook. I have this rice and a piece of meat left over from yesterday. How yer want me do it fer yer?

Prince does not answer. He throws the bat on to the porch. And Mavis crosses over to him.

Doodoo darlin'! How yer want it?

PRINCE [*gruffly*] A pelau.

MAVIS. Creole?

PRINCE. Eh-heh.

MAVIS. Then go round the back there and pick me a handful of peppers.

And again he is the patsy. But he goes off to get the peppers. Pick a lot. I go make it hot. Hot enough to burn off yer mouth.

She goes in. Ephraim sits on his bed smoking and drinking and smiling drunkenly as he listens to the action in the yard outside.

MAVIS [*coming back to the door*] Prince! Prince! Come I akse
   yer something.

PRINCE. Yer see mey gettin' the peppers.

MAVIS. Come I akse yer, nah.

PRINCE. What?

   He comes back around the side of the house.

MAVIS [*confidentially*] Come!

   He moves closer.

   Yer think she had anything to eat?

PRINCE. Who?

   *Mavis indicates the Adams's room with a nod of her
   head.*

   How I must know. Akse she, nah.

MAVIS. Me?

PRINCE. An' yer want to know.

   He calls out as he starts for the Adams's room.

   Little girl! Little girl!

MAVIS. She name Esther.

PRINCE [*going up the steps*] Esther! Esther!

   Esther comes to the door.

   Hi!

ESTHER. Hi!

PRINCE. That girl there want to akse yer something.

ESTHER. What?

MAVIS [*crossing all the way over from her own room she stands
   facing Esther.*

   Yer eat yet?

ESTHER. I've eaten.

MAVIS. That was all I wanted to know.

   And she starts back across the yard towards her room.

   Nobody can't say now that I ent have no feelin'. It got
   too many people 'round here who does give they mouth
   liberty.

   *She goes inside. Prince follows her. Esther remains for a
   moment on the veranda and then crosses to Ephraim's door.*

ESTHER. Ephraim?

73

EPF [*from inside*] Hi.

ESTHER. I can't find anybody home. Ma. Nobody. She told me to be home by three. Now she herself not here.

Ephraim puts the glass and the bottle away, rises and opens the door. As Esther enters the room she picks up some paper off the floor.

If yer want me to—I can help clean up in here for you. Till Ma comes home I don't have anything to do. You seen her, Ephraim?

EPF. No.

Crushing the paper into a ball—she sits on the bed.

ESTHER. Today—you know—we walked part way up Chamcellor Hill—And then we came down through the Botanic Gardens out into St. Anns—and all along Spanish Acre until we got to the resovoir. Last year—You heard?—They found a man drowned in there. When they found him, Ephraim—He had been floating in the water for days and days. Nobody knew. And for all that time people had been drinking the water. [*She makes a face.*] Ma says the reason why nobody knew was all the watchman's fault. He lost his job, Ma said—Right there and then.

Thunder rolls in the distance.

A boy of seventeen calls as he comes into the yard from the street.

BOY. Mr. Adams?

EPF. Somebody out there, Esther.

ESTHER. To me?

BOY [*jumps on to the porch*] Mr. Adams.

ESTHER [*goes to the door*] Oh! . . . Hi!

BOY. Hi. Is your daddy in?

ESTHER. No. Ma isn't here, either. Yer came for the bats?

BOY. Ya. I'm going up to practice. And I wanted to try the new one this afternoon.

ESTHER [*coming down the steps*] I know the one you mean. You want me to get it for you?

BOY. If it's okay.

ESTHER. It's okay!

She runs up the veranda steps and into the house. Ephraim comes down the yard and picks up the magazine and the empty cigarette packet. The boy looks at him and nods.

BOY. Hello'.

EPF. Hi, fella!

The boy looks up at the sky.

BOY. I hope it doesn't rain. It just might though.

Ephraim stands in the doorway looking directly at the boy. But the boy having made his remark has turned away. Esther comes into the veranda carrying the new bat.

ESTHER. Here. Is this the one?

BOY. Yes—that's it.

Taking the bat—he examines it with a professional eye.

ESTHER. You know Jan?—My friend from next door?

BOY. No. I don't think so.

ESTHER. Her brother says that you can make a hundred runs any time!

BOY [*smiling*] Oh?—I wish I felt so!—I'd make a hundred every time! . . . This is okay. Will you give your daddy a message for me?

ESTHER. Yes.

BOY. Will you tell him that . . .

ESTHER. Oh—there's Ma now. Ma-ah. [*Crossing to meet her mother*] Ma, he came for the bats.

Sophia comes in from the street. She is dressed in one of her Sunday frocks. A flowered voile. Her shoes, hat and handbag are also for special occasions. These items are by no means new—but have been well preserved.

BOY. Hello, Mrs. Adams.

SOPHIA. Afternoon, Mr. Murray.

BOY. Esther gave it to me. I hope you don't mind. I—sort of —wanted to use it this afternoon.

SOPHIA. Mr. Adams said they were finished. All but one.

BOY. I'll call back tomorrow, Mrs. Adams. But—I'd like him to know that I was talking to the principal a couple of days ago. Next season they are going to engage a coach for the junior school. I took the liberty of mentioning Mr. Adams's name. The job is his—if he wants it.

ESTHER. Oooh, Ma!

SOPHIA. Thank you, Mr. Murray. I'll tell Mr. Adams.

BOY. He'll have to go through the formality of making an application, of course—but it's more or less settled. . . . You just tell him about the job. That's what's important—I'll explain the rest when I see him. So long, Mrs. Adams. Esther.

He starts to go.

ESTHER. 'Bye.

SOPHIA [*calling after him*] Mr. Murray! Ask yer father to send us the money for the bats as soon as is possible—will you?

BOY. Sure. I'll bring it around later if you like.

ESTHER. 'Bye.

BOY. See yer.

He goes out.

ESTHER [*waving to him*] 'Bye . . . 'bye . . . 'bye. . . .

Sophia sits on the bench.

SOPHIA. Ephraim!

She has no more words.

ESTHER. Ma! Where's Byron?

Sophia is not listening.

Ma! Where's John Byron?

SOPHIA. At Ma Tarvey.

ESTHER. Can I go for him? And, Ma!—Please let me have twelve cents to buy ice-cream?—Please, Ma? Ma?

She realizes that something is wrong.

Ma?—What's happened?

Mavis comes to her door.

SOPHIA. Esther. Esther sweetheart—Come inside. Something I have to tell yer.

Sophia and Esther go into the house.

MAVIS. Like we go have to break a bank!

Ephraim ignores the remark.

Like they can't manage yet to spring Charlie Boy out on bail. Watch out, boy. They might want to borrow yer boat ticket.

EPHRAIM [*angrily*] Five weeks from now. I remember you. I send yer a postcard.

MAVIS. Send it to *them*!

PRINCE [*from inside*] MAVIS!

Her eyes on Ephraim—she turns and goes back into her room. Ephraim goes into his room for his cap.

Rosa hurries in from the street.

ROSA [*calling*] Mrs. Adams . . . Mrs. Adams.

EPF [*coming quickly into the yard. Tightly*] She's inside! Talking to Esther!

The girl stops on her way across the yard. Ephraim and Rosa stand facing each other for a long awkward moment.

ESTHER [*from inside*] No!

SOPHIA. Esther.

ESTHER. No!—Is not true!

SOPHIA. Esther.

ESTHER. Ma!—Oh, Ma! . . .

And she comes quickly on to the veranda and runs into the yard.

SOPHIA. Esther . . . [*As she appears*] Esther—Come here!

ESTHER [*turning on her mother*] Is you! Is you! . . . If Daddy did what you say he did! Is you! Always pushing him and pushing him. And making him feel shame in front of all *kinds* of people. Is you! Is you! Is you!

She screams hysterically at her mother and runs off along the street.

EPF [*after a moment*] I think I'll go drive that last trolley.

Ephraim has gone.

SOPHIA. You heard her? Is me. She says is me. I been slavin' to keep things goin'. I been. . . .

ROSA [*crossing to Sophia to comfort her*] She didn't mean what she said.

SOPHIA. I been tryin', Rosa.

77

ROSA. Esther knows that.

SOPHIA. You talked to Mr. Mack.

ROSA. He said . . . He said the matter was out of his hands.

SOPHIA. As if I didn't know . . . Everythin' happenin' wrong.
Wrong for me. Esther. Charlie. Wrong for you . . . What
you going to do about Ephraim?

ROSA. Let him go.

SOPHIA. You want me to talk to him?

ROSA [*crossing to her door*] Let him go! Wedding-rings too
cheap to have to kiss one man foot for.

SOPHIA. Men funny sometimes. Even after they come out the
church at times—they ent sure. Yer should a seen Charlie—
them first days—with me. Rosa—Sometimes yer got to
stifle pride. Think about the child growing in yer insides.

ROSA. That Ephraim!—He was the only one!—But he teach
me good!—Now I'm ready for anything!

SOPHIA. Don't talk so. Yer sound like Mavis.

ROSA. I ent fillin' my eye with water fer no man.

SOPHIA. Rosa—I always was pickin' on Charlie. But I know
the many times he was worth a bowlful of tears. Look little
Esther—just gone out there. Her heart breakin' right now
for him.

She has crossed down into the yard.

ROSA. Mrs. Adams . . .

*She follows her and puts a hand on Mrs. Adams's arm in
an attempt to console the older woman.*

Mrs. Adams.

But it is Rosa who breaks and bursts into tears.

Sophia puts a pair of comforting arms around the girl.

SOPHIA. Is awright, child. Is awright. Now who yer crying for?
Esther? Charlie? Or me?

ROSA. Nobody! Nobody!

The thunder rolls. Closer now.

SOPHIA. Hush. Hush . . . Listen. Is beginning to rain.

*Sophia looks up at the sky and as the lights go down rain-
drops crackle—then come tearing along from distant rooftops.*

78

*In the darkness we hear the storm. Then the last wash of rain
and a roll of thunder grumbling itself away.*

Act Three

SCENE 2

*It is evening. The rain has stopped. And the night is fresh and
cool.*

*Ephraim, dressed in a shirt and light-coloured slacks, com-
pletes his packing. On the bed are some face towels, a couple
of heavy sweaters, a few American magazines, a* Readers Digest,
*two hard-cover books. He wraps a pair of shoes in a bit of news-
paper and puts them into the holdall. A zip-front windcheater
jacket hangs over the back of a chair.*

*The little portable radio on the bureau is playing a selection of
Sinatra records.*

*Out in the yard—Prince—leaning on the gate—listens as
Sinatra sings 'Polka Dots and Moonbeams'.*

PRINCE. Mavis! Mavis!
    Ephraim gulps a drink.
MAVIS [*from inside*] Eh-heh!
PRINCE. Yer ready?
MAVIS. Eh-heh!
PRINCE. Well, I waiting . . . Oh God! The old Sinatra! Let the
    world take Bing!
    *The light goes off in Mavis's room. And Mavis—dressed to
    kill—comes out into the moonlight.*
MAVIS. Yer make up yer mind yet which club we going to?
PRINCE. A new one. The Scarlet Flamingo.
MAVIS. Where that is?
PRINCE. Cumana.

MAVIS. That so far!

PRINCE. So it far!—We walkin'?

MAVIS. They have good music?

PRINCE. We could always leave. Yer like mey shirt?

MAVIS. It could pass.

Mavis sweeps by Prince, and they exit up the street.

In the distance the clock on the tower of Queen's Royal College begins to chime. As Ephraim checks his watch, the street lamp is lighted, and Sophia enters from the street. She walks up the veranda steps. Her shoes are damp. Her flowered dress hangs limp. Her hat—soaked from earlier rain—now sit even more comically on her head. She has been walking the streets, looking, searching, asking for Esther.

SOPHIA [*opening her door*] Esther? . . . Esther?

She goes into the house. The light goes on.

Sophia comes back into the veranda. She takes off her hat and puts it on the table. Reeling in the clothes-line, she begins removing the remaining pieces of clothes. She takes a few pieces down. She stops. Looks over towards Ephraim's room. Crosses the yard and calls to him.

Ephraim?

EPF [*going to the door*] Mrs. Adams?

SOPHIA. Can I talk to yer?

EPF. Come in.

SOPHIA. I not disturbing yer—I hope?

EPF. Here—sit down. I'll move these.

He pushes some articles aside and Sophia sits on the bed. Ephraim goes to the bureau, takes up a bottle and pours her a stiff drink.

SOPHIA. Boy—I'm cold! Tired an' cold! The rain wet me! It dry on me!

EPF. Mrs. Adams—Here—Drink this—Yer soon feel better.

SOPHIA. Why Charlie had to go do a thing like that? . . . I just come from the station. They let me go in and tell him good night. . . . You see Esther?

EPF. No.

SOPHIA. Since I tell her this afternoon—she run off—She ent come back. I been searchin' high and low. Nobody like they see her. Young people don't know, nah. They don't know. Yer think Esther could feel more shame than me? The least she could do is come home.

EPF. Drink the drink, Mrs. Adams.

Sophia gulps the drink.

SOPHIA. So *you* goin'? Rosa tell me this mornin' and I couldn't believe. And this afternoon I want to talk to yer—Yer walk off.

EPF. I had was to work, Mrs. Adams.

He has begun to pack his toilet articles.

SOPHIA. Yer plan this thing, boy. Not a soul yer tell?

EPF [*rising*] Mrs. Adams. A man will be comin' here in the mornin'—to take away the bed an' a couple of other things. Anything yer find will come in useful—Yer welcome to it....

He unplugs the radio.

Tell Esther—the radio is fer her. An'—I have a couple of ties here that Charlie might well like.

SOPHIA. Ties?—Fer Charlie?... Epf!—What about Rosa?

Ignoring the question—Ephraim returns to his packing.

Ephraim!—Yer go walk off and leave her here?... Ephraim! I'm talking to you!

EPF [*exploding*] Mrs. Adams! I akse yer something! You know fer certain sure—you want a whole lot more fer Esther—than you ever had a chance to get! My ole man was *nothin'*!... He used to drive a transport mule-cart! Everybody stinkin' dustbin!—Hawk!—Spit!—Crap! Is so funny—Yer find I want something better for meyself!

SOPHIA. Yer have it, Ephraim!

EPF. Have it?

SOPHIA. Soon they would have made yer inspector!

EPF. Today I told them they could *shove* that, Mrs. Adams!

SOPHIA. You're a fool! God—you're a fool! Yer have a future here! An' yer shoving it aside!—Fer what? To go off where? What's wrong with allyer? Ephraim—I born and grow up

81

in this Trinidad. I see it change. I see things open up—
Making room fer young people. Young people like you.
Take Esther. When I was Esther's age . . .

EPF. NOT NOW, MRS. ADAMS!

And then softer—with some concern:

Mrs. Adams. Look—I don't have the time. Here. Look,
This is ten dollars. Tomorrow it help yer get a lawyer talk
in court for Charlie.

*Sophia can only look at him. He throws the money on the
bed.*

[*Defensively*] Nobody else but Charlie could of get them ten
dollars from me. Mrs. Adams—A taxi will be here in a
minute. If yer don't mind—I just want to finish up in here.

SOPHIA. This afternoon—you was ready almost to involve
yerself fer Charlie. Why?

*Ephraim has shut himself off. Rising, Sophia picks up the
ten-dollar bill, crushes it and drops it on the floor at Ephraim's
foot. She moves towards the door.*

SOPHIA. Finish up. Finish up. Finish up.

*Rosa has come out of her room to fill a lemonade jug at the
water tap. As the water spills into the jug Sophia hurries to
the door.*

Esther? [*And seeing it is Rosa*] Oh!

ROSA [*turning to her*] Good night, Mrs. Adams.

SOPHIA. Good night, child.

Rosa enters her room.

SOPHIA [*turns back to Ephraim*] Rosa is home!

Epf says nothing.

Boy—you heard me?

EPF [*quietly*] Mrs. Adams. Concentrate on yer own affairs.
Leave me to attend to mine.

*A car has pulled up outside and the driver calls from the
street and then comes hurrying along the alley-way.*

DRIVER. Ephraim! . . . Ephraim! Hey, Ephraim!

EPF. Joe!

He gets to the door as the light goes off in Rosa's room.

DRIVER. I'm here, man. I'm here.

EPF. A few minutes, pal—an' I with yer.

DRIVER. Fifty miles to go, yer know.

Ephraim comes back towards his room. Sophia stands blocking his path.

EPF. I have to go, Mrs. Adams!

SOPHIA. Ephraim!

EPF. I got to go!

SOPHIA. Rosa pregnant! Fer you! Yer know that—Don't yer?

He moves forward, forcing his way past her into his room. Sophia follows.

No! You jest not goin' to walk out of here an' leave that girl! She has no mother—no father. Nobody in the worl'! Only you! Months now yer twining yerself round she—strangling she—till she can't see nobody but you. Now she tell yer she makin' baby—yer goin' off on a boat! Yer don't want to know!

EPF. Mrs. Adams!

SOPHIA. I want you to go out there! I want you to go out there right now! Tell that man yer ent going no place!

EPF. Lady, yer know what yer sayin'? Yer know what yer tellin' me to do?

SOPHIA. What in heaven name! This place yer runnin' to! Have fer you!

EPF. Lady—You would never understand!

SOPHIA. No! I not bright like you!

EPF. Mrs. Adams! Move away from the door! [*And losing all patience*] MOVE AWAY FROM THE DOOR ! ! !

SOPHIA. B'JESUS CHRIST SOMETHING GOING TO GO RIGHT IN THIS PLACE TODAY ! ! !

EPF. I have a taxi waiting, Mrs. Adams!

SOPHIA. LET IT WAIT ! !

The taxi horn sounds. Exasperated by her stubborn interference, Ephraim allows the heavier bag to drop to the floor. He sits on the bed. Sophia moves into him.

The time! When you first asked Rosa! And she didn't know

what to do! Was to *me* she come! As if she was my own daughter! I had to tell her *how*! So that you could be the first!

He tries to go past her and she grabs hold of him.

That girl come to this yard straight out of the orphan home. Them nuns have her so—She don't know nothin' 'bout men. Then you come. Yer start makin' eyes at her. She fall fer yer. Yer make her lay-up on that bed NIGHTS with yer!

EPF. SHE LIKED IT, LADY ! !

SOPHIA [*slapping him across the face*] MORE THAN YOU? And now yer takin' up yerself to go off God knows where! —To leave her alone in this stinkin' yard. Yer know WHAT will come of her?

EPF. TO HELL WITH IT ! !

He pushes her so that she crashes against the bed and falls.

I don't give a damn! No blasted woman go TRAP me here!

SOPHIA. Is no trap! Is true!

EPF [*grabbing at the suitcase and holdall*] So what? The baby born! It live! It dead! It make no damn difference to me!

And he is already in the yard as the driver hustles in again from the street.

DRIVER [*shouting*] That tanker ent go wait all night, yer know!

EPF. TAKE ME OUT OF THIS BLASTED PLACE ! !

Ephraim tosses the holdall to the driver, who catches it.

DRIVER. Let's go!

EPF. GO !—GO ! !—GO ! ! !

Rosa's door is thrown open—She rushes into the veranda— her body naked under the shawl. She calls her man's name —'Ephraim'! But he is gone.

Out in the street the taxi door slams shut. The engine starts up with a roar and the lights are switched on. The taxi moves away. The noise of the engine dying in the distance. Sophia comes down into the yard. She moves towards Rosa.

SOPHIA. Rosa. He gone. But don't mind. Perhaps—Charlie get over this trouble. Perhaps he get the coaching job. The baby born. We help look after it for yer.

84

Old Mack—calls from Rosa's room.

OLD MACK. Rosa? . . . Rosa?

The girl turns and goes in.

SOPHIA. O God! . . . No!

Sophia starts up the veranda steps. Esther comes in along the alley. She stops as she gets to the gate.

ESTHER. Ma-ah!

The call has warmth—a certain immediacy—strength. It should give the impression that the future could still be hers.

And then we hear the last trolley as it hisses by out on the road.